Visual Signals

Issue One

I0480468

JULY-SEPT 2020 ISSUE

KITE0080 & MTHU Update

What's up my future friends?! This is KITE0080 of Musics the Hang Up.

A lot has changed since the last issue. I moved to Dogpatch, San Francisco. I have my own apartment after 7 months of living at home with my Dad. My brother had his second child, Emilia! I went through a semi heart break and rekindled old friendships. I'm currently on a 41 day meditation program that requires me to do 30 minute meditation and 20 minute yoga, as well as wake up before 6am and take cold showers (we'll see how it goes).

My new job is a contract job and they told me that I now must limit my hours to 40 hours a week, so I have a lot of free time alone in a brand new closed down city. Because of this I've rekindled a friendship with my last Chinese teacher, Yuchi. She's the best, we talked often in the past but now I'm feeling like our friendship has hit a new high. I'm happy that I can get on phone calls again without mentally blocking myself at my fathers. Oh, she even submitted an article for this issue~ Regardless, I've signed up for a bunch of classes with 4 teachers on italki. I'm back on my Chinese learning grind. My teacher Vincent is crazy, he's from Taiwan and he sounds like a radio announcer. So when he speaks it's super clear and when he speaks English it just cracks me up. I'm loving it.

I also bought a strumstick or a 3 string guitar like instrument. It just felt the cold in these white walls I'm living in. I could use some live music. It's easy enough to play and it'll keep my entertained.

The second book in my N1 Galaxy Series will be release at the end of August as the preorder ends the 27th. It's a sci-fi novel about *Quinn Comfort*, a programmer who has recently been captured after leaking a government conspiracy. He's holders give him a new body, a new job and identity but his real destiny lies in saving the world from a deactivating virus. How does he escape his new architecture job and get back to programming the world? Find *Unlimited Knowledge* on Amazon~

As for Musics the Hang Up specifically, there's not much going on. I'm still posting daily releases on the front page of the website. I don't really have any plans for any videos or where the direction is going but Visual Signals is now my main focus. I'll explain why in an article below. Part of taking Visual Signals to the next level, I bought the domain, http://visualsignals.xyz, at the moment it's a simple landing page but it'll be the new domain of future updates about this project and were to read digital versions of articles that do not make it into this book.

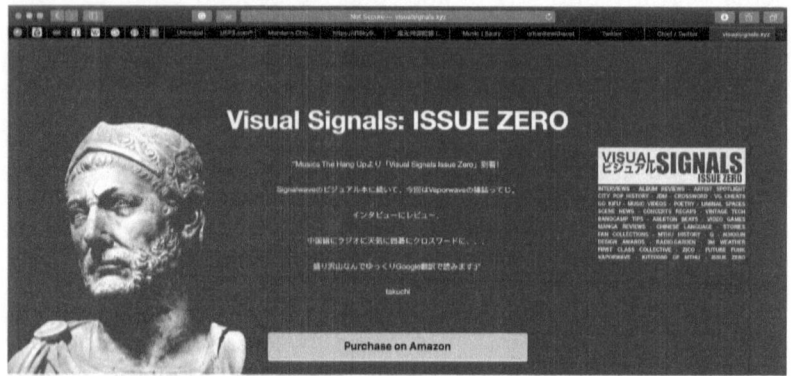

Things are feeling good in my life. I am happy with my new path and move to SF. I don't exactly have future goals at the moment but I do love publishing books. I love being an author and I want to thank everyone who has bought any of MTHU books or any of my other releases. It's an amazing feeling to accomplish something, print it and hold it in a physical form. It's been a while ride and I am happy to be back. If I never had that 40 hours a week limit put on me, who knows when I would have returned to MTHU or Visual Signals! Let's turn this project into what it deserves to be.

As always, if you want to contribute to the next issue hit me up at contact@musicsthehangup.com or dm me @signalsvisual

Cheers,
KITE0080

Follow This Project on Twitter:
@SignalsVisual

Hyperconsumersim by Harsh Noise Mall

By Jay Wallace // @jaywallace1

Vaporwave tends to overlap with other ambient/experimental genres like Dark Ambient, Plunderphonics, and Hypnagogic Pop, but one genre crossover you don't see much of is Noise Music, specifically Harsh Noise Wall: A cacophony of noise, consisting of static, field recordings and/or music compositions stacked on top of one another, rattling your eardrums and vibes at the same time. Harsh Noise Wall sounds like the exact opposite of Vaporwave, almost incompatible... then Harsh Noise Mall proved that wrong with "Hyperconsumersim."

Released by Xanadu Sounds in 2019, then given a cassette release by Hairs A'Blazin' in July, Harsh Noise Mall's "Hyperconsumersim" is an anti-Mallsoft album. Two tracks, each 22 minutes long, layered with "the claustrophobic sounds of a crowded shopping mall," per HNM's description. Children's excited shrieks, squeaks of people's shoes, their distant, incomprehensible voices drowning each other out, a barely-heard Muzak track echoing from somewhere, and then every so often, a security alarm pierces the din of hyperactive, unending commerce, almost bringing relief and order. Towards the end of the second track, this constant "swirling" noise subtly appears, only adding to the unease "Hyperconsumersim" gives you. It's too much, there's too many people, I got to get out of here. And then... it fades away in an instant. Not exactly a chill Saturday evening at the mall hanging with your friends.

Some could say "Hyperconsumersim" isn't Vaporwave, it's Noise Music, but not me. HNM has made an album that leans on the ironic, critical side of Vaporwave. It just doesn't have any icing, so to speak. The Vaporwave scene tends to swim in nostalgia of the '80s and '90s, where commercials and music of that time promise that you could just buy your happiness. People remember the music, the toy stores, the Orange Julius, but not the crowds, the security guards, or the hassle to get new dress shoes for a function you don't want to go to. That's why I bought Hairs A'Blazin's cassette on a whim; "Hyperconsumersim," as aggressive as it is, is a reminder of what that time was actually like, or at least felt like when you couldn't go to KB Toys.

T e l e p a t h like ambiance

I recently bought a cassette copy of birth of a new day by
T e l e p a t h and to this day I am so captured by the atmosphere
each track gives off.

Like many fans of the album, the ambient reverb totally steals the
show for me. So I had to investigate how to replicate it in
Ableton.

There are two Audio Effects
we'll be playing with;
standard Chorus and
Reverb. It'll probably be
easier to just look at the two
screenshots and replicate
them but I'l try my best to
explain the theory here.

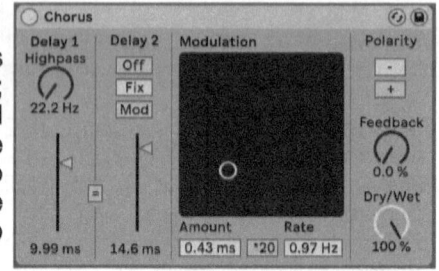

First in Chorus, alone just gives off full sound to any sample. The
thing is the second the sample ends the chorus ends. So we'll
need an additional audio effect to keep the sample moving.
That's where the reverb kicks in. With a longer Decay Time, the
sample will hold out for as many seconds as you input. Longer
the Decay Time, longer the sample reverbs. Additionally I like
making ambient sounds like this more wet as it gives more echo/
reverb.

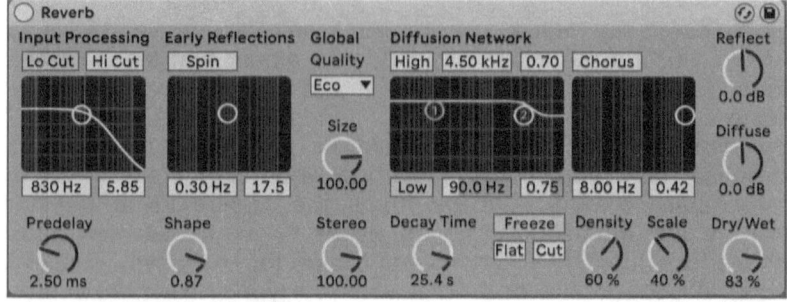

I think I am pretty close and I hope you can try it out on a pad or
melodic sample.

PIZZA MEMU

コロナウイルス対策の期間中テイクアウト箱代無料と

会計時 PIZZA10%OFF にて提供いたします　※税込み価格です

トマトベースのピッツァ

①マルゲリータ・・・・・・・・・・・・・・・・・・¥1,250
（トマトソース、モッツァレラチーズ、バジル）

②ロマーナ・・・・・・・・・・・・・・・・・・・・¥1,450
（マルゲリータ＋アンチョビ、オレガノ【香草】）

③マルゲリータアズーリ・・・・・・・・・・・・¥1,500
（マルゲリータ＋ゴルゴンゾーラ）

④マルゲリータ　エ　サラーメ・・・・・・・・¥1,500
（マルゲリータ＋サラミ）

⑤マルゲリータ　エ　パンチェッタ・・・・・・¥1,500
（マルゲリータ＋ベーコン）

Pizzeria　Alto　Palazzo

Waifu Radio 2 Review

By Nekkun // @n3kkun

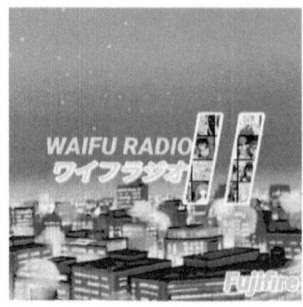

FujiFire's Waifu Radio 2 is one of the first albums I think of when someone says "Future Funk" or "Anime Wave". It has everything you're looking for in a future funk album such as lightly sprinkled side chain for flavor, soft and hard cuts to feed your hip hop needs, Japanese sampling that feels fresh and new even if you've heard the source material, and those classic fade in and outs with the filters on them. The only thing this album is missing is a heavily accented name drop by a female voice over at the right moment. You are now listening to FujiFire.

What really draws me to this album is the perfect mixture of Future Funk and Anime Groove. FujiFire really makes this album live up to its name. The track Do It For Love and Falling in Love (feat. Strawberry Station) shows that FujiFire really knows how to make a classic Future Funk hit. Add in the seductive song Kawaii Disco Fever (feat. Anipai) to see the other mastery in this album, Anime Groove. You even get your experimental sounding bops

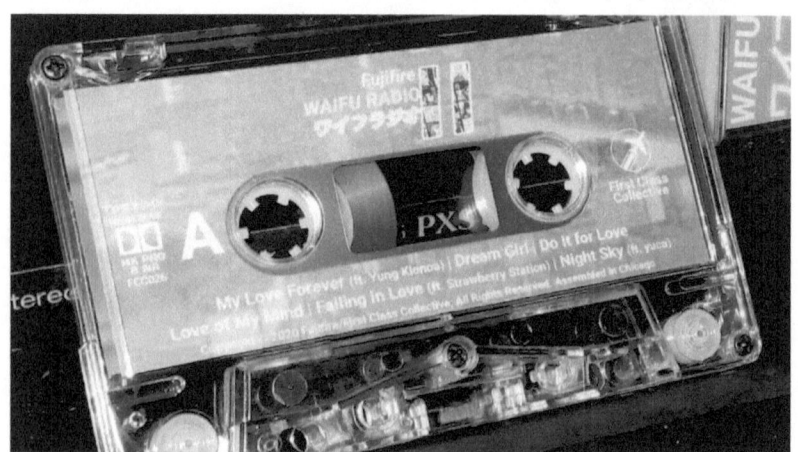

like *See your Face* coming into play, which has become one of my favorite songs on this album.

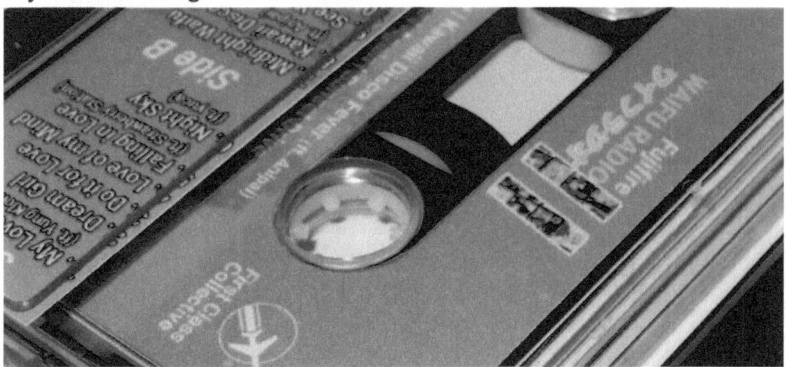

The folks over at *First Class Collective* know what they're doing. They are dubbed, printed, and labeled the cassettes from one of the most inspirational DIY setups I've ever seen. They even have some super secret Dolby tools to help improve the sound quality and get the most from their setup making the DIY tapes feel professionally dubbed. These are definitely high quality.

This was a great album to listen to all the way through. I really like the work put out by FujiFire for this one and I really hope this will come out on more physical media sometime in the future. I know I'm not the only one. You can find FujiFire on Twitter, Bandcamp, and Soundcloud for more fresh jams!

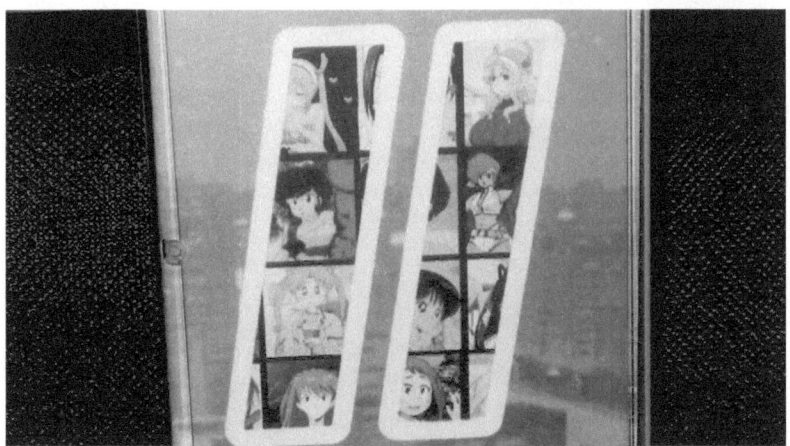

Tape Collection - Eric Roy

By Eric Roy // @RobertEricRoy

Nyetscape – After

Early vapor artist with a track on seminal The Eternal Dream System compilation, this is the only full-length physical release by Memphis TN's Nyetscape. On Lo-Fi By Default (Now That's What I Call Seapunk), it's top-notch. If you're looking for something to scratch that classic mediafired/eccojams itch, this is it. Nice 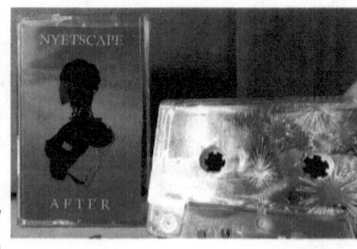 holographic silver tape where little fireworks explode slapped on one side of a TDK D60 is a nice touch too.

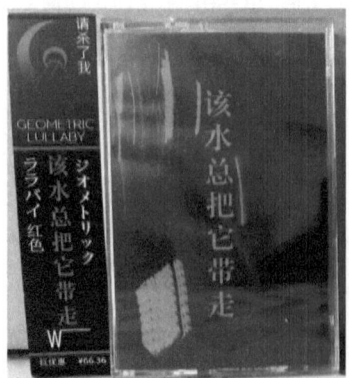

W⁻ -- 该水总把它带走

Dark-ambient meets neo-classical, but in a word: cinematic. The OST to a movie not made, yet you watch it alone, again and again. With physical releases routinely selling out (latest offering GEO-064 in 15 seconds), Geometric Lullaby is known for impeccable design and curation. One run of 25 on GeoLull (as opposed to the regular 50), along with the fact Brooklyn's Watching Waters is a longtime favorite (with tapes still available at bandcamp??) makes this a crown jewel in the collection.

AcMafee-Education — Textbook Oregon

A short EP filled with new age samples and field recordings around Oregon whose climate famously jumps from jungle forest to mountain peaks to arid desert, the music herein does the same—vaportrap, future funk, utopian virtual, and eccojams can all be heard in the scant 10 minutes of music. The clean art is what drew me in. Can't go wrong with Seikomart, as anyone who's received a package hand-crafted by Lumi will know.

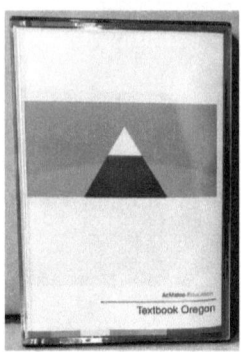

Network Superhighway --

With ties to Negative Plus, Hantasi, TDS and SOCECO, this one's hard to pin down. Produced in an uptempo synthwave fashion with video

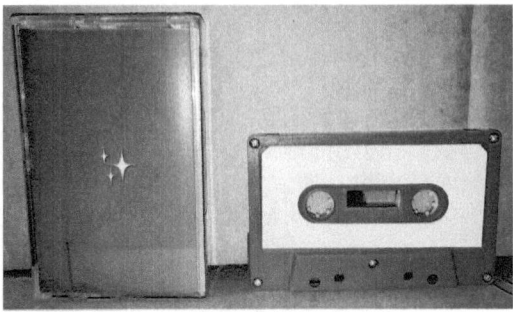

game samples (!) back in 2016, this one dances and parties with no one else around. An early label collab between Sud Swap (SS056) and Seikomart (S&M009), they only made four of these, condemning it to obscurity--a crying shame for a release sounding so good.

Television Experience (テレビ体験) -- Y. 2089

This is the "Friends & Family" version, although some were sold publicly. One of David Russo's aliases (over 50 including HKE, DARKPYRAMID, Subaeris), Y. 2089 has a sweeping, improv feel to it akin to Casino Master (another project) but with more of an "early vapor" mood. Jcard resembles vintage Fuji "AXIA" PS-I packaging from 1985. On the excellent and experimental Tokyo Exchange label.

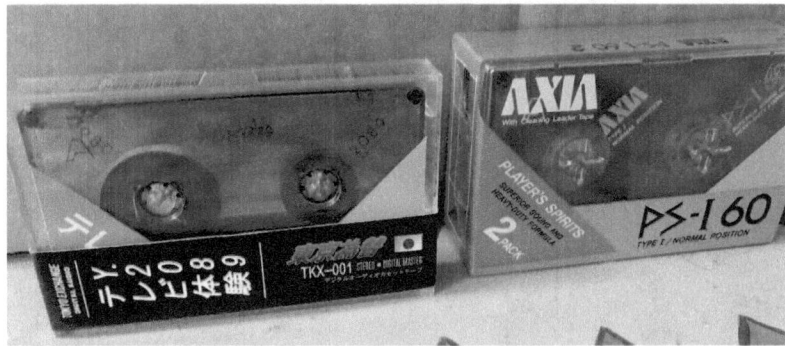

KITE0080s Thoughts: *I am totally amazed at Eric's collection and I'm grateful to have him share these with us.That Y. 2089 cassette has been on my wishlist since the first time I saw it and I couldn't believe I met someone who had it. I love the aesthetic of all of these Thanks mate~*

Songs That Hit Differently

August Edition

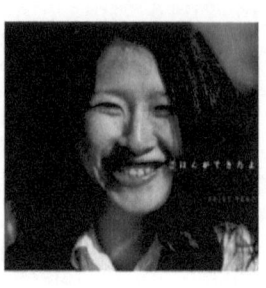

1. Akiko Yano - COLOURED WATER (1980) [right]
2. So Nice - Love Sick (1979)
3. 南無阿彌陀佛聖號 - Jade Video
4. deca joins - 海浪
5. 拍謝少年 Sorry Youth - 兄弟沒夢不應該 Brothers Shouldn't Live Without Dreams [below]
6. 昏鴉 - 週六的你在週日死去 (my weekends)
7. Citizen - Jet
8. wind96 - Feather Lakefront
9. Modern Baseball - Just Another Face
10. 万能青年旅店 - 乌云典当记
11. Gil Scott-Heron - Small Talk at 125th and Lenox
12. Disclosure, Fatoumata Diawara - Douha (Mali Mali)
13. 猫シ corp - 東京 haze (extended tape version)
14. Days N Daze - Fuck It
15. 陳綺貞 - After 17 (oh my youth TT_TT)
16. Fazerdaze - Lucky Girl
17. Hip Hop 1995 XIII Instrumentals (Youtube it, it's vibes)
18. Wait a Minute! - Willow Smith (guilty pleasure ngl)

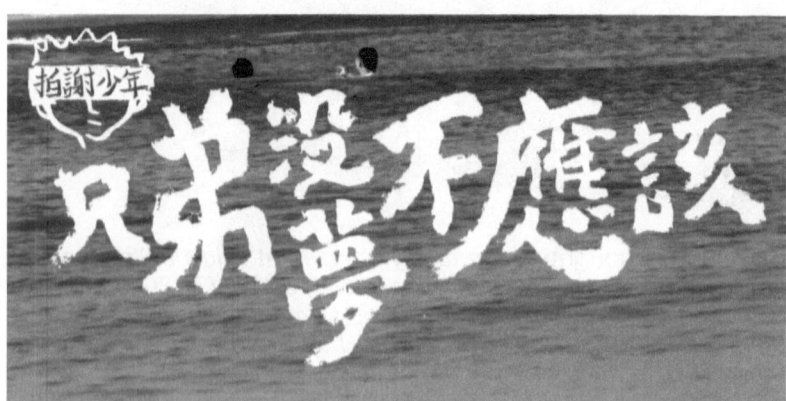

Now Available On Amazon!

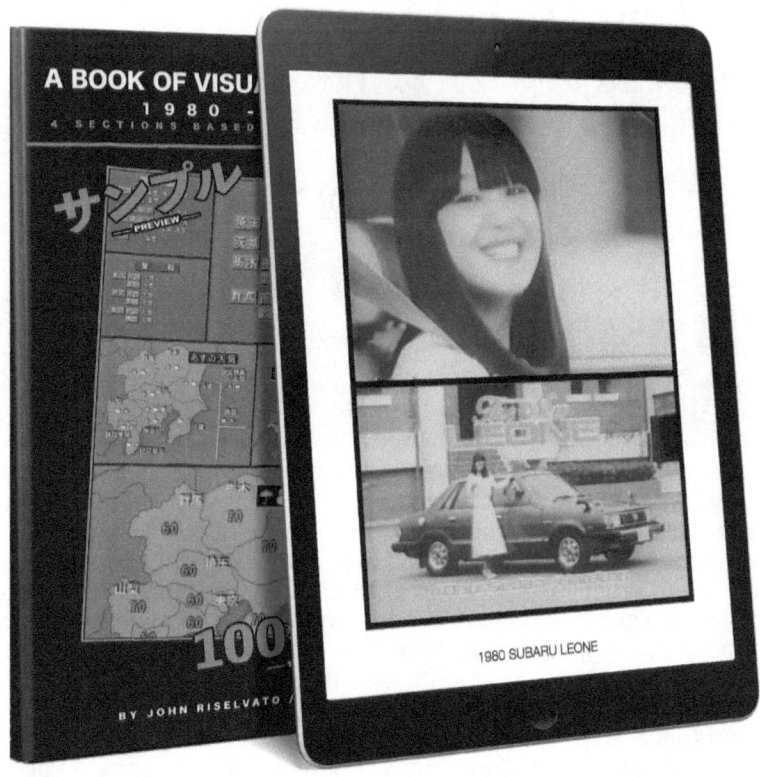

1980 SUBARU LEONE

"A Book of Visual Signalwave" is the experience, feels and emotions found in Japanese television from the years 1980 to 2001. The world of Signalwave and its music has always had a visual side. This book is a contribution to the music genre in a different way with a focus on a period of time, the commercials, tv and cars. This book is pure Signalwave for the eyes! Over over 90 pages of commercials turned into comic book form. Each commercial should be viewed as an individual art piece that evokes emotional ties felt in Vaporwave.

Available in Paperback and Kindle
*Size may vary from advert

Past Concerts

S L U S H W A V E   2 0 2 0

August 15th, Vapormemory hosted Global Pattern's Slushwave

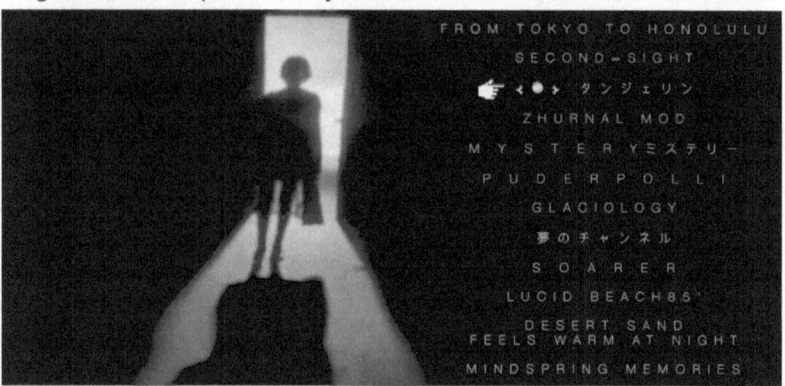

FROM TOKYO TO HONOLULU
SECOND-SIGHT
👉 ◀●▶ タンジェリン
ZHURNAL MOD
MYSTERY ミステリー
PUDERPOLLI
GLACIOLOGY
夢のチャンネル
SOARER
LUCID BEACH85'
DESERT SAND
FEELS WARM AT NIGHT
MINDSPRING MEMORIES

2020. Hosting sets for 12 slushwave artists and in-between sets interviews. I stuck around for the 猫 シ Corp. interview which he went over some details about working with Telepath, his experience running his label and more. After their conversation, a new slush artist for me, Zhurnal Mod, came on and totally blew me away. Their aesthetic is super high fashion but extremely chill. Perfect dream shopping sounds. The stream made me a new fan

VAPORSPACE STL X AQUABLANCA

Vaporspace STL has really be crushing it on the digital concert grind. For those who don't know, Ronny is usually running Vapor shows in Saint Louis but of course all that is on hold, so it's natural to see him pushing the boundaries of the digital world. I hope he's still dancing at home.

Regardless, this concert holds a special place in my heart, as my favorite signalwave related label finally put on a concert. It was amazing to hear 天気予報 live, listen to

14

Winterquilt and chill with sleeparalysis. Plus they donated proceeds to the ACLU (American Civil Liberties Union). If you haven't checked it out, all of Vaporspace STL concerts should be available on Twitch, so check them out.

WAVEPOOL BY MONTAIME

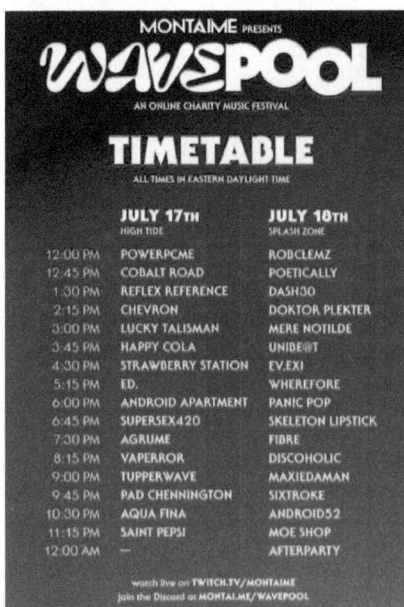

MONTAIME PRESENTS

WAVEPOOL

AN ONLINE CHARITY MUSIC FESTIVAL

TIMETABLE

ALL TIMES IN EASTERN DAYLIGHT TIME

	JULY 17TH HIGH TIDE	JULY 18TH SPLASH ZONE
12:00 PM	POWERPCME	ROBCLEMZ
12:45 PM	COBALT ROAD	POETICALLY
1:30 PM	REFLEX REFERENCE	DASH00
2:15 PM	CHEVRON	DOKTOR PLEKTER
3:00 PM	LUCKY TALISMAN	MERE NOTILDE
3:45 PM	HAPPY COLA	UNIDE@T
4:30 PM	STRAWBERRY STATION	EV.EXI
5:15 PM	ED.	WHEREFORE
6:00 PM	ANDROID APARTMENT	PANIC POP
6:45 PM	SUPERSEX420	SKELETON LIPSTICK
7:30 PM	AGRUME	FIBRE
8:15 PM	VAPERROR	DISCOHOLIC
9:00 PM	TUPPERWAVE	MAXIEDAMAN
9:45 PM	PAD CHENNINGTON	SIXTROKE
10:30 PM	AQUA FINA	ANDROID52
11:15 PM	SAINT PEPSI	MOE SHOP
12:00 AM	—	AFTERPARTY

watch live on TWITCH.TV/MONTAIME
join the Discord at MONTAI.ME/WAVEPOOL

For minute, WAVEPOOL was literally the biggest thing since the original release of Floral Shoppe. It seems I couldn't go anywhere during the week of July 17th without someone talking about it, retweeting hype or even exploding about how good it was afterwards. However MONTAIME was able to pull it off, let's just say a lot of other digital concerts have envy. And how couldn't they with artists like Saint Pepsi, Moe Shop, VAPERROR, and so many more, it's like a dream come true if it was an IRL concert. I can't imagine what it's like for my boys EV.EXI, Strawberry Station, and Android Apartment to go from playing Groove Horizons in London to playin digital shows with Saint Pepsi. They really did make it!

Honorable mentions:
1. 100% Electronica presents: Beyond The Virtual Utopia Experience
2. HausMo x ESS Quarantine Concerts
3. Space Age 5G AM Radio ~ Æscape Sounds (which was amazing dreamscapes when I tuned in)
4. Vaporspace Culture Worldwide (Aug 28th & Sept 4th) with Vaporspace STL
5. First Class Collectives Discord VHS party for their first VHS, *First Class Collection: Volume Two*

夜晚男朋友 - 噢

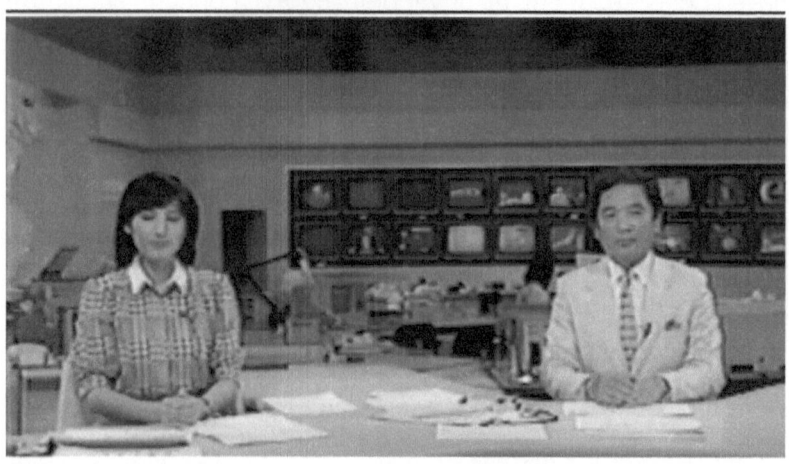

If you look outside your window tonight, the starry sky will remind you of a sighing boy. A boy who once stood upon his traditional tiled roof. A memory of where he grew up in. The building his parents had built. The parents who slept peacefully, unaware. The wind may blow and the sky might look innocent but for the boy upon his 2 story home, he stands at attention begging the moon for answers. Standing in reflection, Quiet and peaceful but not with the answer he wanted. It was the darkness below him that really knew the ending. The darkness kept away thanks to his friendly moonlight. Metal rusted nails. Nails that should have been as tightly held as the boy who eventually fell...

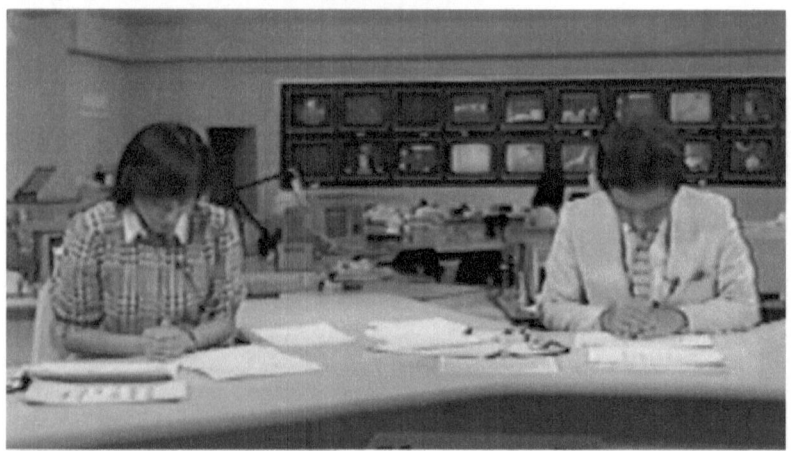

MTHU x 100% Electronica

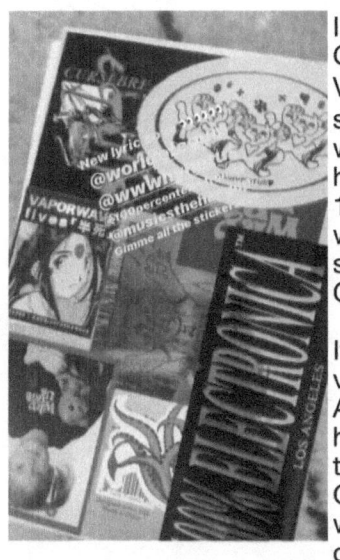

I don't know exactly how Negative Gemini was able to get one of my Vaporwave Lives 「半死」 stickers but she recently *instagrammed* a post with it on her new lyrics book. I know how one of them made it into the 100% Electronica household. So what better time to share the cringy story of KITE0080 meeting George Clanton for the first time.

It is 8/31/2019 and the first ever vaporwave festival is in full force. After George does his ESPRIT set, he heads to the back of venue to meet the fans. At the time I had yet to meet George personally, but I wanted to wait for the crowded fan group to die down before I introduced myself. I'm not that interested in meeting him, but I wanted to tell him thanks for setting up the show and that if he ever needed anything let me know. So I walked up to him and said just that. But it came off like I was saying if he needed anything to make ECON smoother, which he responded something along the lines of, "Just enjoy the concerts." Classy dude. Did I mention he knew I was KITE0080 of MTHU before I even introduced myself? Maybe I was starstruck all of a sudden but the cringe was just starting.

We met for two seconds, I didn't really have anything to say anyways, I didn't want to waste his time. So he goes over to a chair and sits to the left of a merch table (I think Christtt was manning at the time). I forgot I had these *Vaporwave Lives* 「半死」 stickers so thought I should give him one. So I walk over to were he is sitting and hand him a sticker like a professional asian man. Two hands on a business card style. Full bow and everything. "Here's a sticker," I said & walked away after he said thanks. Why!!! It was so subservient feeling.... Anyways, I hope that's the same sticker on NG's new notebook and it made my life of embarrassment worth it.

New & Noteworthy

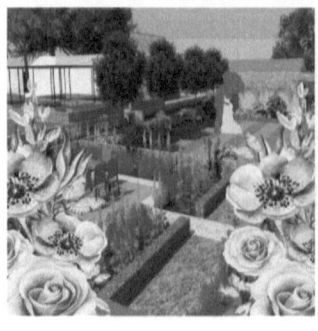

A Morning Mood
by Subliminal Network

Originally released April 21, 2020 , this classic vapor album is reminiscent of strolls in a garden with the one you love. The first track, L o v e   i s   a   b e a u t i f u l   t h i n g, takes you through an expertly crafted hedge maze of peaceful mystery. What new flower or bird will you discover next? Throw this album on this weekend while you spice up a breakfast for you love. They'll fall for you all over again.

フードコート P O R N O
by Nanoshrine

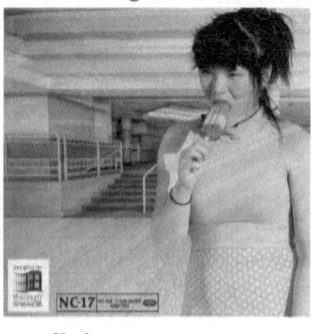

The instrumentation (or if it's sampling) is amazing. Very heavy 80s synths with these upbeat melodies that are driven by percussion that leads the way, but doesn't over power it. Some how this album has been under the radar even after the cassette release, which is a shame. Don't let the name scare you off from an awesome album. Inside is pure smooth optimistic vapor jams, and if it's a dirty mag, it's the classiest of the options.

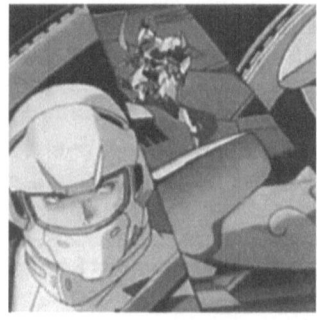

NEW EARTH: GENERATION X7 by W.R.I.

Ever since first finding Future Funk because of Macross, I always felt like the mecha side of vapor has been under developed. So any chance I can get to find a new release that gives me those old childhood Gundam or Big-O vibes Is awesome. Interestingly this uses Chinese anime samples and is on the chaotic mash of sounds & samples side of things. But the sound works really well. It put W.R.I on the map for me.

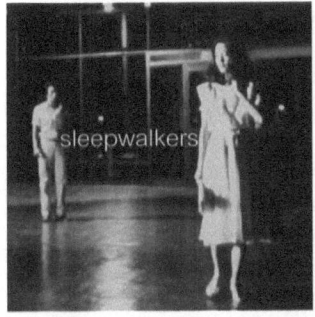

sleepwalkers by Murochka 闇黒

Although the album art might give off stalker vibes, inside you'll find some of the most romantic late night sensations. In a lot of ways, this is a shining example of someone (like myself) listening to vaporwave and thinking, oh it's got to be so easy to make vaporwave. Then when I try it, it doesn't sound nearly as classic. This has the method down and we are better off because of it.

ENERGY by DESCO RADIO-CLUB EP

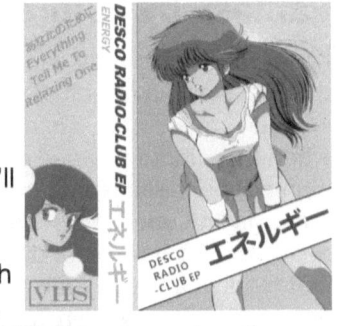

If the album art drew you in, then you'll be happy to know the music inside is just as *attractive*. Although only 4 tracks, the album is jammed back with future funk and Japanese disco feels.
Although this isn't DESCO RADIO-CLUB's most popular album, it shows how they've evolved with each release. Gotta give it to them for their album art aesthetic. We need more of these on actual cassettes.

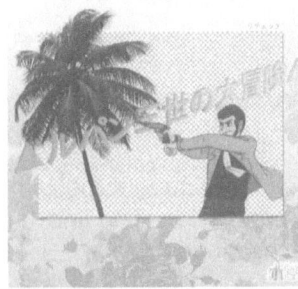

▲ルパン三世の大冒険▲ by ラチェック

Obviously, anything with Lupin is going to be sly, cool and full of action, right? Well... this album isn't what you're expecting. It's a mix of break beats, hyper active splicing but with vapor elements. Oh and did I mention this is from 2014? There's deff some pushing the boundaries on what vapor is, it even has tastes of Signalwave. If you only listen to one track, check out *WINDOWS98*.

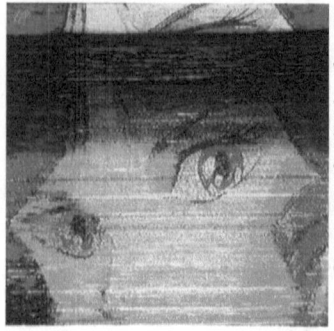

e n i g m a 謎 by Spear 槍

The album feels so suppressed and full of emotional VHS dreams. Like the music wants to burst out, but due to the weathering of time and the heads on that old player not being nearly as strong, we get what is left over. The mastering on this is unbelievable.

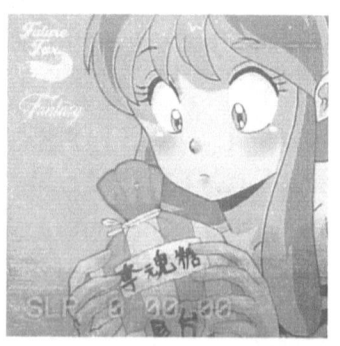

Fantasy by Future Fox

I'm at this point in my vapor career that I'm starting to actually get drawn in when I see Lum… Thanks Zico. So when this album popped up I had high hopes, because no one has really given Lum the justice she deserves. So how did it do…? The first track is a future funk edition of none other than Mariya Takeuchi's *Plastic love*. The second track and final track? Another generic future funk track, least this time I don't know the sample. It seems Future Fox has dropped from the scene after this album as it was their last release (2019). There is potential here, just still feel like Lum could really use some more love.

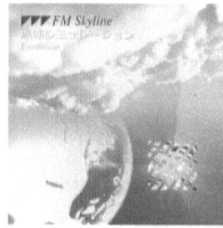

FM Skyline body:texture render

Bonus: This single track really caught me with it's OS like samples, amazing bass line and flutes that could make the clouds dance.

Scene News

An End to a Street Fighter Legend
In early August, Street Fighter Executive Producer, Yoshinori Ono // @Yoshi_OnoChin, announced his resignation with the company after 3 decades of working with the company. These days he is best known for his public image in the competitive "World Warriors" series as well as keeping the brand true to the series. I'm not the biggest fighting video game fan but it's always sad to see industry legends step down. If you want to read his full statement, it is available on his twitter (above).

Chuck Persons "Ecoojams Vol. 1" turns 10!
In the month of August we are celebrating the 10th year anniversary of Chuck Persons "Ecoojams Vol. 1", which is just crazy to be writing. It paved the way for a lot of future vaporwave styles and established the Megadrive, underwater aesthetic seen to this day. The team at VA:10 Association put together a tribute album, ECOO:10, with over 51 tracks and artists coming together to celebrate. What a monumental moment!

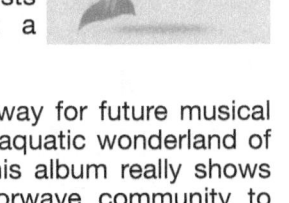

"Eccojams Vol. 1, notoriously paved the way for future musical styles by captivating its listeners with an aquatic wonderland of mystery and nostalgic tones. We hope this album really shows the passion and dedication of the Vaporwave community to collaborate together and bring forth something to honor the legacy in the best way possible" — Chief // @Chiefahleaf

MTHU Hits 1k Subs on YouTube
Big number, but there's no celebration. More of a footnote. Thanks everyone who got me here and I hope I get the motivation to make videos again so your sub isn't useless. I have some ideas but I need to get established in my new life first. Until then, expect Visual Signals to be my main project. Wow, 1k people like me! Sort of, my videos still get like 100 views after a month. Yet some how books like this get a lot of interest. I must not have the YouTuber personality.

KissAnime and KissManga get DMCA'd

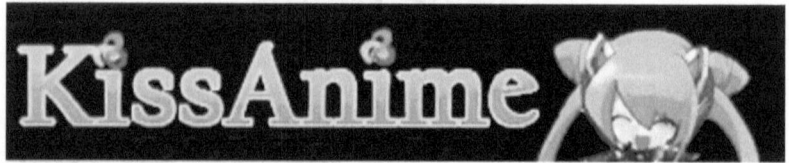

Saturday Aug 15th, was a sad morning for the pirate anime fam as they went to access their episodes and were presented with a single sentence, "All files are taken down by copyright owners. The site will be closed forever. Thank you for your supports."

Every bookmark, every episode, every ounce of data was wiped in the matter of minutes as a DMCA took down their videos and image files from Google Drive, their primary hosting service. With Google complying with the take-down, there's not much the Kiss team could do.

For those who lost their bookmarks, I feel for you. It's like we all lost a good friend. This has happened before in the past but it took 3 months to get the servers back online. There might be hope but it seems the team is rather demoralized or maybe there's a huge legal battle ahead if they attempt to bring it back. What ever happens, it was good while it lasted. We really need a Netflix for anime already. Cheap, easy to access and does everything these piracy sites do but with less ads and faster servers. We can all dream.

The KissCommunity discord is still live as of this writing, so if you have questions or just want to hang with the community, here's the invite: https://discord.com/invite/eCzUxNB If you visited on the day of the DMCA, Everyone was paying respects on the discord with massive emoji reactions on staff posts. It was a heartfelt and emotional scene.

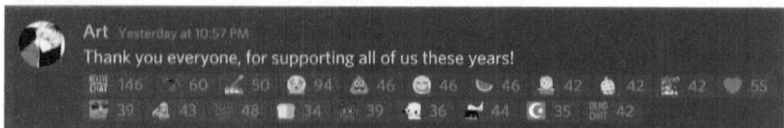

Got news?
Did we miss any news or have something to announce for next month? Send us an email at contact@musicsthehangup.com

Nichijou 《日常》

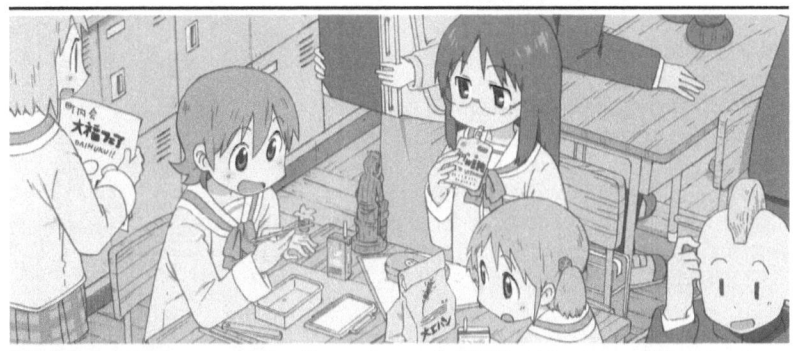

Nichijou has to my favorite anime of 2020. What was first just an interested in the art style quickly turned into me laughing my butt off for hours! I've never seen such chaos and endearment in my life. A slice of life never felt so intense! @Dezonator described it on twitter as, "Nichijou is chaotic peacefulness," and I completely agree. So let's look into the first few scene you can watch on YouTube to introduce you to the anime.

1. **Nichijou - My Ordinary Life - Safe!!**
   In this scene Yūko Aioi explains how she saves her favorite part of her lunch for last so she can end the experience with a "Yum!" Just as she says this, a sausage shaped like a little octopus pops out of her chopsticks and the extreme sport of saving that little piece of meat turns into an action packed, "Don't let it touch the floor at all costs," event. I won't spoil how it ends but let's just say, the penny on the floor made me laugh so hard.

2. **Nichijou - Mio Loses It**
   In this clip, a police officer asks Mio and Yūko if they know anything about someone who might be using counterfeit bills on the vending machines. Yuko denies knowing much but Mio starts to act suspicious. The officer describes the same designer bag as Mio, and Yuko is starting to second guess if she has anything to do with it. Surprisingly, what is inside her bag is worth knocking out 2 grown men, Yūko and a goat. Seriously, the animation here is incredible and so funny. Can you guess what's inside?

Casio AE1200WH-1B

Year Introduced: *2000-present*
Display: Digital
Size: 45mm Case Diameter
Backlight: amber

My latest fascination has been cheap Casio watches. I haven't bought any but if I had an extra 25 USD, the *Casio AE1200WH-1B* would be it.

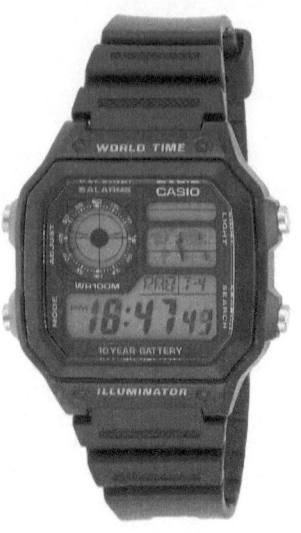

I'm an all black kind of guy, most of my clothes are black, my shoes are black, etc blame it on my emo roots but when I first saw this watch, it caught my eye for the lack of color. It's sleek and solid without the blues or reds of its older brother. The tans and white do not detract from the minimalistic feel but adds tiny accents with purpose.

Which brings me to the complicated yet beautiful additions on the upper half. The circle is called a digital dial, which has multiple features depending on display. The first is a compass, it's always nice to know which way is north. It also can be used as a countdown timer, and probably more, the details online are rather limiting.

To the left of the digital dial, a green filled map is displayed allowing you to cycle between timezones quickly with the digital display.

There are 5 timers in it, military and regular time, silver buttons, a an orange backlight, and so much more. What's not to love?

Maybe the greens and tans are a little too flashy for you, well Casio knew you existed and made the AE1200WH-1A. Same face, same features just pure black and white. Oh and half the price!

LONG LIVE BB64

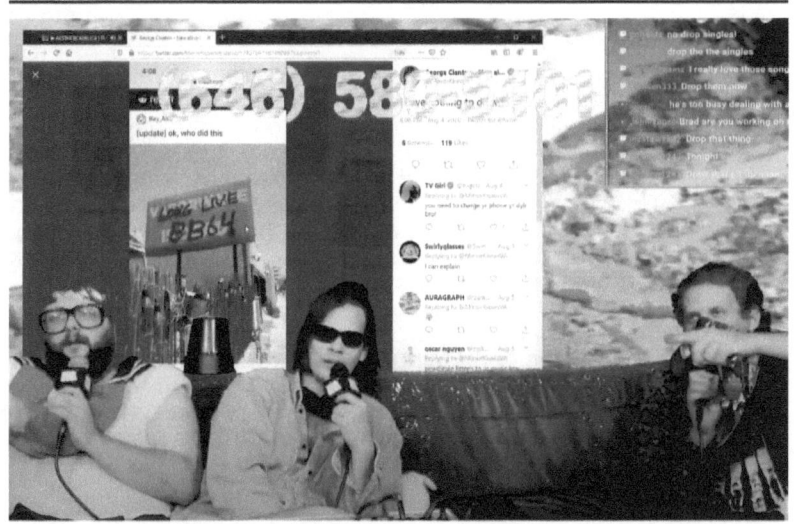

In early August someone defaced the famous pink and teal LA, "Vaporwave is Dead" billboard with a "Long Live BB64". It was announced on *100% Electonica's THE BIG STREAM #22 w/ TV Girl* that BB64 was BLOODbath64 AKA TV Girl (seen right). He personally hopped the fence, got up on the ladder and tagged some subpar graffiti. What was the point? It seems to get his side project (released August 3, 2020) some hype.

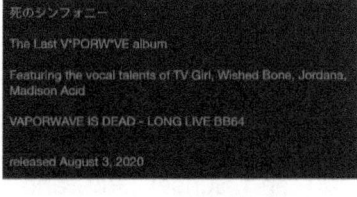

AESTHETICADELICA by BLOODbath64 can be found on Bandcamp and might be released on VHS with 100% Electronica, cause apparently they have an in-house analog system. I don't know how I personally feel about it but it got him on 100% stream and people talking about vaporwave again. At least the album is mint.

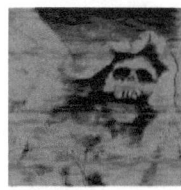

Listen / Purchase here: https://bloodbath64.bandcamp.com/releases

FOMO

By maki // @maki44875987

As much as I try, I can't make a clean break from physical media. I've been collecting things since I was young, starting from probably Garbage Pail Kids cards and working my way up since then. I was really hitting my stride in the early 2000s, when I had a ton of disposable income and a computer that connected me to eBay. Things died down for a while, but once I found vaporwave, that collecting bug reared its head again. So many beautiful vinyl splatters, colorful cassette shells, and artwork waiting to complement my collection.

I generally take a careful approach with my purchases now – asking myself if this is something I'll truly want to keep, or I'll buy to support the artist. I can't (and never really did) buy something just to buy it. I'm sure I'll miss a ton of releases, but that's completely okay. I've been able to purchase things I wanted and am continually impressed by the talent in the scene. There is absolutely no way anyone could keep up.

Our current state, this culture of immediacy and instant gratification, is both a blessing and a curse. Social media brought us the concept of FOMO (fear of missing out), but we can also search around the internet to find those samples we just can't place. I wasn't around for the "early days" of vaporwave, but I can still find a lot of the old stuff on Bandcamp.

Anyone can go and grab terabytes of space for relatively low cost, allowing a very low barrier to entry for someone to start building a formidable library of vaporwave releases. You could spend a day downloading the entire catalogs of Business Casual, DMT and Sunset Grid, and you'd still be barely scratching the surface of what the vaporwave scene has to offer. Some of the best music being made right now, maybe five people have heard it. You're not missing out on it, though – the fact that it exists is beautiful enough.

Artists have pulled albums, labels have disappeared. It's all part of the scene. There is absolutely no way to capture the entire world of vaporwave and what it has to offer. We're talking a decade of content, with tons of music coming out daily (how many email notifications do you get about releases?), and that's only what's known. Does one "miss out" on all of this? It's a safe bet that we've all missed dozens of albums that, if played for us right now, would make us say, "wow, this is amazing."

One beauty of vaporwave is these artists, discovering these sounds, and using them in such a way that makes the listener "discover" those same sounds. The joy of the producer finding a great sample is passed on to the listener in the joy of finding their reinterpretation. The creators are crate-digging, and with that so are the listeners. Let the cycle be this. There is no way we will ever hear everything, even if we had all of it. Rather than the all-you-can-eat buffet of downloading everything from every source you can think of, curate your collection, keep it intimate, call it yours.

Can you truly miss out on something you never knew about? And even if you did miss it, doesn't that add to the experience, the culture of vaporwave? Missed opportunities, missed lifestyles, missed generations, missed technologies, missed dreams. Vaporwave nearly embraces missing out. You should, too. It makes the things you do find and experience that much more special.

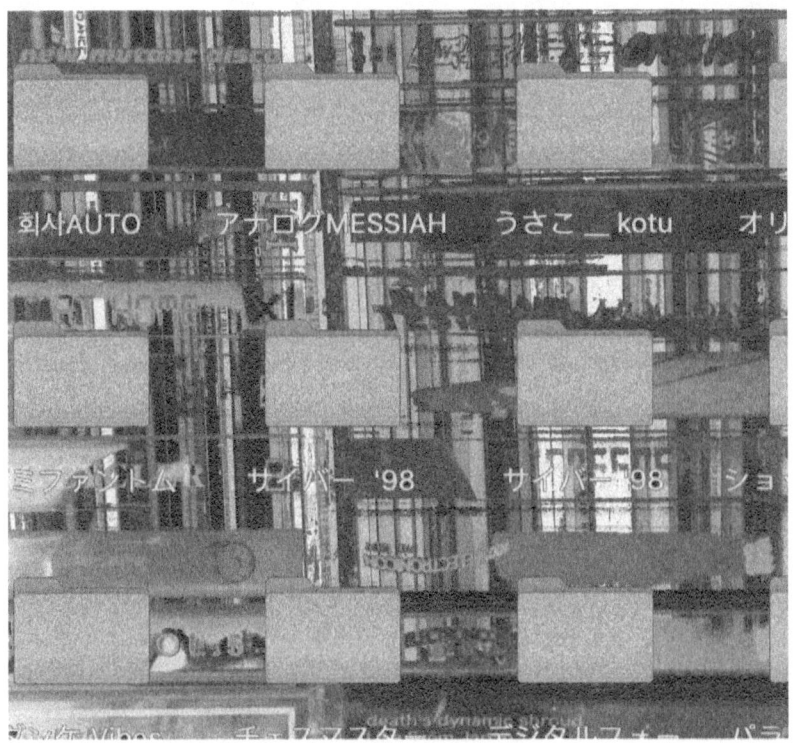

City Pop History - So Nice

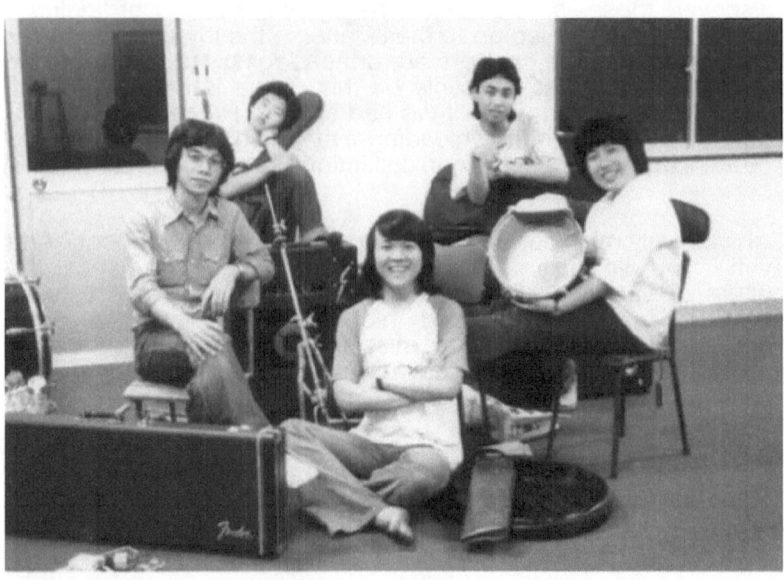

Some times the sweetest sounds come from the most forgotten people and that could have been the case for the amateur city pop group, *So Nice*. When their first and only album, *Love*, was released in 1979, it was more a college band, Barely remembered.

But then in 2013, Love was re-issued on vinyl and I'd like to think thanks to the resurgences of city pop, this album blew up on Youtube and years late gave them the credit they deserved. I love this type of slice of life coffee house music and grateful to have accidentally found it~

Track List:

A1 Sonice
A2 光速道路
A3 Last Kiss
A4 陽だまり
A5 Tight Night

B1 Love Sick
B2 かけぬける風
B3 Earth Mover
B4 別離（わかれ）
B5 Dancing All Night Long

Zojirushi NS-WAC18-WD (review)

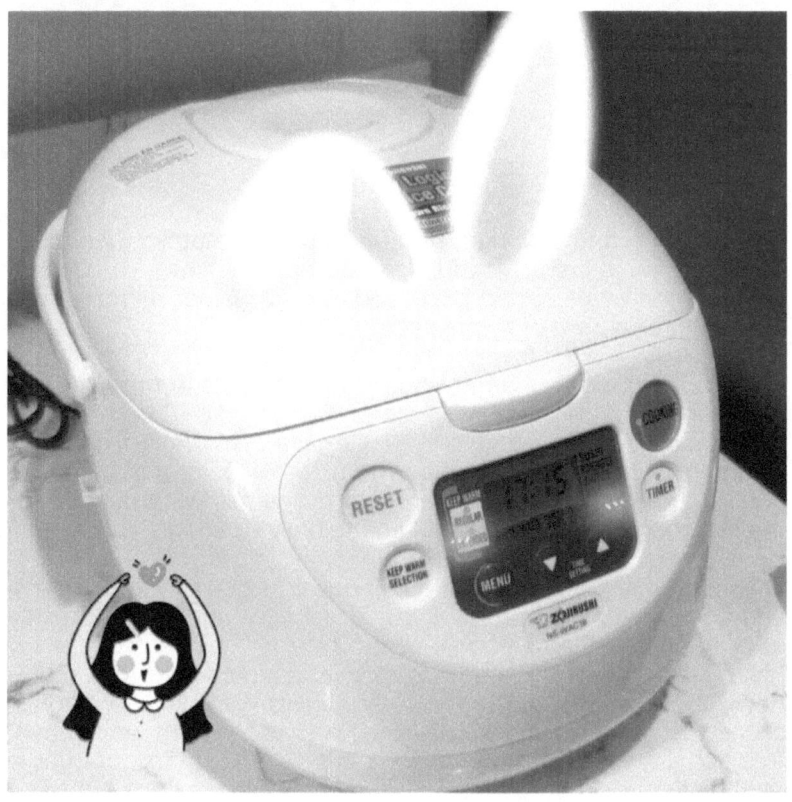

Now that I've moved into my new apartment, I needed a rice cooker to survive on my budget. I'm trying to keep my expenses to the minimum and thanks to my 3 year stent in china, I know how to live well with a bowl of rice and some veggies.

I ended up buying a Zojirushi rice cooker because of a single review, (next page). It's such a touching write up as I am still conflicted about where I am going in my life and what I once had. I joked with my sister but I'll be taking this one to the grave with its Amazon prime price of $136.49 (normally $185.00).

☆ ☆ ☆ ☆ ☆ **The only perfect thing I own**
Reviewed in the United States on February 9, 2020
Color: White | Size: 10 cup   Verified Purchase

Nothing in my life is perfect. Nothing gives back 100% if I treat it right. Everything, everyone, occasionally fails me or falls a little short.

But not this rice cooker.

If you follow the instructions, it will perform without error every single time. Every single grain of rice will be cooked to perfection.

If only everything was like this rice cooker.

When buying a rice cooker, I prefer to own something Japanese and Zojirushi is just that. Plus look at that aesthetic! The lack of corners, the oval-shaped body and a display that mirrors itself. It's beautiful in perfect symmetry.

So it looks good, but what about the rice? At the moment and foreseeable future, I am living alone. So why did I buy a 10 cup rice cooker, I don't know. Maybe I'll have a big family one day. Apparently, it's normal in Japan (and other asian countries) to prolong the life of the rice over night to the following day. So for the first run, I opened up the lid and to my surprise...

Yeah it cooks rice perfectly. I put in one cup of washed white rice and 1.5 cups of water. Took about 30 minutes and I had perfectly cooked rice. I left about half a cup in "warm" mode while I ate my first meal and when I came back a couple hours later for another bowl, the rice was warm, moist and there wasn't any crusty or burned starchy remains. Just good pure cooked white rice. Additionally, the steam hole at the top did not over flow or bubble out like some cheap cookers. Which personally means a lot as I have less clean up.

I wasn't expecting it to take nearly 30 minutes to make one cup of rice but with that knowledge, I won't start cooking the vegetables and tofu so quickly. With a dash of soy sauce and some sriracha, I had a wonderful first dinner with my new life long Zojirushi rice cooker. I suppose next I'll try the rice porridge setting one of these mornings.

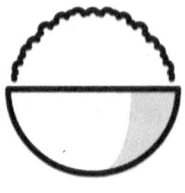

ありがとうございました~

Upcoming releases

Below are some upcoming releases announced publicly on Twitter. Quoted exactly from the artist or label:

1. eventual infinity // @eilogin: *"My album "departure" comes out tomorrow (Aug 21) on Pacific Plaza Records."* (right)
2. Civic Duty Records @CivicDutyRecord: *"New maxi-single by @SidekickWave tomorrow, new @KagoTangerine album next Wednesday"*
3. Dezonator // @Dezonator: *"My release comes out the 28th (Aug)"*
4. Aldo Lazcano // @GrooveRemote: *"August 25th is the release date (for Guest Mix: My Pet Flamingo MegaMix)"*
5. 現實VR // @VaporReality: *"Artist : 卧铺欢迎 Album Name : Causeway Bay Release Day 29th Sept 2020"*
6. Petridisch / Fish Prints // @petridisch
   1. *08.24.2020 - suchamazingdoge - "Crest"*
   2. *09.04.2020 - Contriva "Tell Me When +"*
   3. *09.25.2020 - Cryostasium "Project: 00" remaster/reissue*
   4. *09.2020 - Petridisch "Amaranth Loops"*
7. peter peterlini // @iverprin: *"My album Cerulean drops 09.04 thru GalaxyTrain Tapes!"*
8. flagnjektilo // @injektilo_huy: *"Injektilo - Suburbanism"*
9. Z.E.R.O | 暗闇DESTINY // @iamZEROmusic: *"09.18, my French House-influenced Future Funk record, 'Reload!' is going to be released through Business Casual!"*
10. b l u e s c r e e n // @TylerEllis18:
    1. *"Panorama Capsule" by Zima Clearmalt*
    2. *"West Babylon" by ako*
    3. *"Underglow" by SINOS*
    4. *"愛の波" by 世界は80年代に終了しました*
11. Kanga Corp. // @Kanga_Corp: *"4th of sept - Deadmac's The City on cassette"*

Thanks everyone who responded to Tweet asking for Sept releases. In future issues, I'll ask again to build a massive release list for the next issue as well.

The Rise of Indie Anime

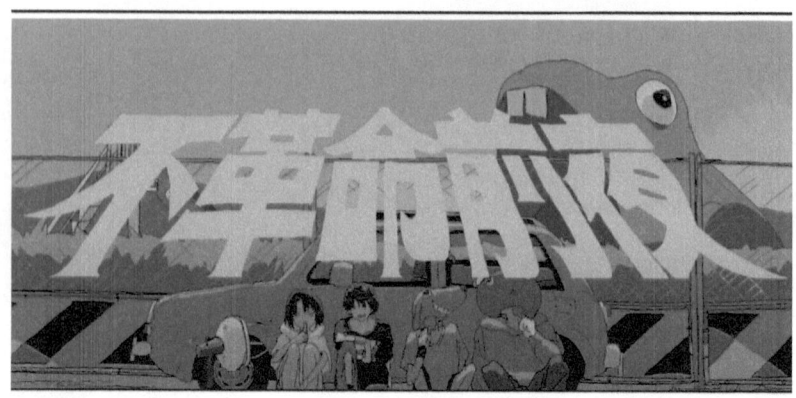

(Above) 不革命前夜 by NEE

Recently, I've noticed a recurrences of the twitter tag #indieAnime in the Japanese animation community. Although still a small group, the animations these artists are putting together are incredible. The first thing you'll notice is most of the animations are either for music videos or just 30 second clips of these incredible worlds they're building.

Some times the artist releases new scenes to their previous uploads or show WIP but I increasingly keep getting impressed. I am happy to see sort of a *"flash animation" days* pop back up again thanks to animation software on iPads, like RoughAnimator or Procreate. It makes me want to get back into animation again. Really cool stuff.

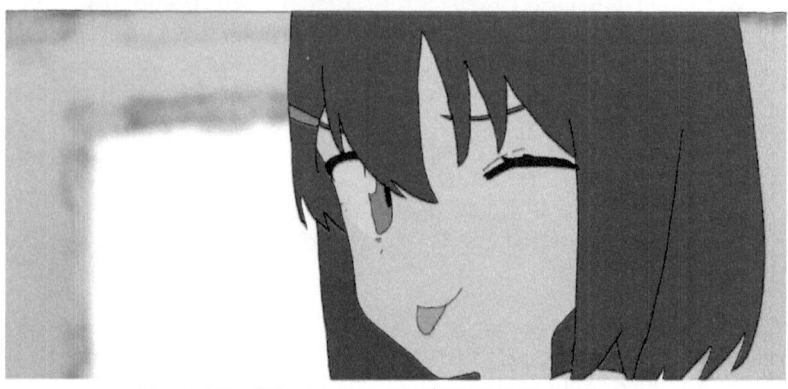

(Above) カフェ店員の女の子 by こむぎこ2000 // @komugiko_2000

GTA: Liberty City Stories (PS2)

WEAPONS
- Weapon Set 1 – UP, SQUARE, SQUARE, DOWN, LEFT, SQUARE, SQUARE, RIGHT
- Weapon Set 2 – UP, CIRCLE, CIRCLE, DOWN, LEFT, CIRCLE, CIRCLE, RIGHT
- Weapon Set 3 – UP, X, X, DOWN, LEFT, X, X, RIGHT

MONEY
- Get $250000 – L1, R1, TRIANGLE, L1, R1, CIRCLE, L1, R1

RESTORE LIFE
- Restore Armor – L1, R1, CIRCLE, L1, R1, X, L1, R1
- Restore Health – L1, R1, X, L1, R1, SQUARE, L1, R1

WANTED LEVEL
- Increase Wanted Level – L1, R1, SQUARE, L1, R1, TRIANGLE, L1, R1
- Wanted Level Never Appears – L1, L1, TRIANGLE, R1, R1, X, SQUARE, CIRCLE

PEDESTRIAN
- Random Pedestrian Outfit – L, L1, LEFT, L1, L1, RIGHT, SQUARE, TRIANGLE
- Pedestrian Riot – L1, L1, R1, L1, L1, R1, LEFT, SQUARE
- Pedestrians Attack You – L1, L1, R1, L1, L1, R1, UP, TRIANGLE
- Pedestrians All Have Weapons – R1, R1, L1, R1, R1, L1, RIGHT, CIRCLE

QUALITY OF LIFE
- Faster Gameplay – R1, R1, L1, R1, R1, L1, DOWN, X
- Slower Gameplay – R1, TRIANGLE, X, R1, SQUARE, CIRCLE, LEFT, RIGHT
- Perfect Traction, Down=Car Hop – L1, UP, LEFT, R1, TRIANGLE, CIRCLE, DOWN, X
- Cars Drive On Water – CIRCLE, X, DOWN, CIRCLE, X, UP, L1, L1
- Destroy All Cars – L, L1, LEFT, L1, L1, RIGHT, X, SQUARE

けいたいでんわ 3G

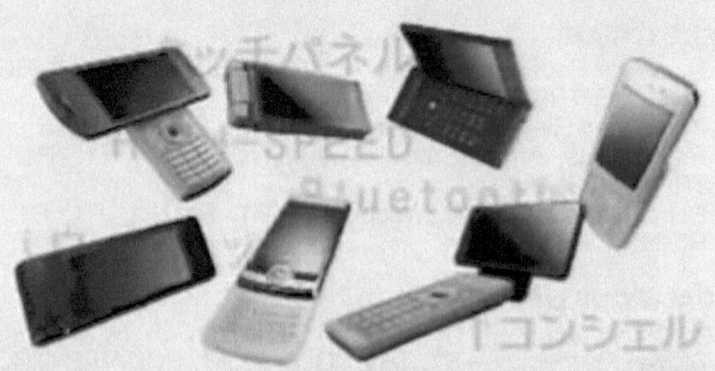

Maplestory Archer (Java Mobile)

Back when mobile phone screens were the size of a thumb print, there were small pixel art games with the slowest refresh rates capturing our attentions. See back in the day, we didn't have app stores or game libraries that were easily accessible, we had to search the internet for hidden gems that works on our tiny blackberry pearls (my first cellphone).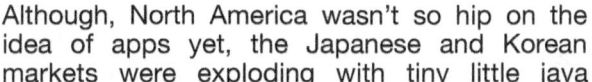

Although, North America wasn't so hip on the idea of apps yet, the Japanese and Korean markets were exploding with tiny little java games and of course they would make it into the hands of weebs like me. One of my earliest memories with my Blackberry Pearl was changing that little track balls color (it had an LED under it) and installing a little game called *Maplestory Archer*.

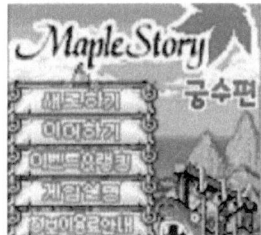 Maplestory at the time was one of the biggest MMORPGs on the internet. If you weren't playing Runscape, you were out on MS killing slimes and trees admiring the level 100s that killed every enemy on the map for giggles. So when I found out there was a mobile version I could sneak and play while in class, I had to install it.

I don't remember if the game had any english, but that didn't matter, those Korean developers had already installed in me how to play the game. Start off with a primitive weapon and hack and slash my way through leveling. It wasn't an online game, nor did it really feel like Maplestory but the sprites fit and imagination ran wild.

It's actually pretty difficult to find any information about this game and it makes you wonder, is anyone out there collecting these old java mobile games? I know there were other gems I played but no long can remember the names of. Maybe it's just another part of technological history that will be lost in bytes be remembered by childhoods.

Unlimited Knowledge (book 2)

I'm recently published on Amazon the 2nd book in my sci-fi series and wanted to share a little except of Chapter 4~

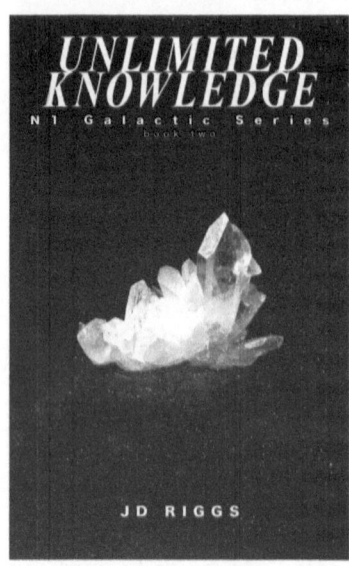

I don't know how she knew who I was without my introduction but I did like the customer service aspect of it. Like a child in a candy store for the first time, I decided to stick around and experience the full complimentary amenities. Inside another woman welcomed me by name and asked if I was interested in seeing a menu.

Inside a beautiful luxury lounge with a full bar and various tables. It was furnished with the latest modern designs and high ceilings, black and white with splashes of orange; very high society. I was the least well dressed in the room but I blended with the air of wealth and business. Around me, Businessmen chatted over cocktails and picked at cheese platters. I smiled, "Yes please. If I could request it, can I sit near the back window?" I asked, pointing to the floor-to-ceiling window that overlooked the shuttles taking off.

"Quite good taste sir, best seat in the house," she responded and took me through the dining room.

The song 東京 HAZE by 猫 シ Corp. played in the background as I carelessly browsed the menu. I artificially fit this new high fashion world but "who was I really?" I caressed the white glossy finished table. My fingers met with the condensation ring around the glass. I painted the water towards me and a memory flashed in my mind. The 3 water lines looked like a design of a bank building I had seen on J-27. It must have been an artificially generated memory by my new skill set. This actually got me excited to start practicing my drafting skills. I decided as interesting as the vip packing was, I wanted to dive into my new life. I was scared but I needed to stop delaying the enviable...

Learn Chinese - HSK 1

I've been learning Chinese for 3 years now. Everyone starts with HSK 1, here are the next 27 to get your introduced to the beautiful ancient language (Part 2).

一	yī	one
二	èr	two
三	sān	three
四	sì	four
五	wǔ	five
六	liù	six
七	qī	seven
八	bā	eight
九	jiǔ	nine
十	shí	ten
零	líng	zero
个	gè	one, a, an or measure word
岁	suì	year
本	běn	volume
些	xiē	some
块	kuài	piece
不	bù	no

Try it yourself: 我是十一岁。我要一本书！不要两本书。。。

Official MTHU Merch

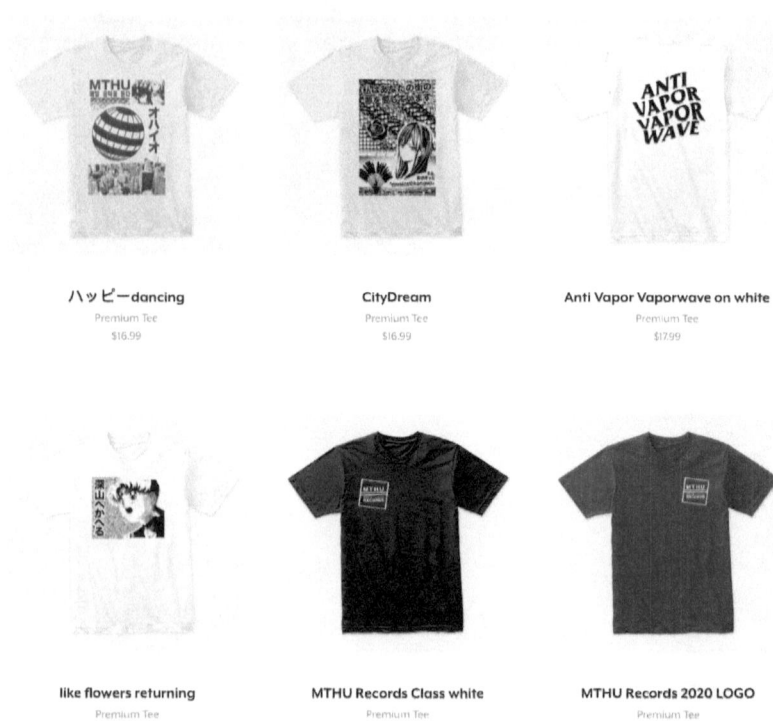

ハッピーdancing
Premium Tee
$16.99

CityDream
Premium Tee
$16.99

Anti Vapor Vaporwave on white
Premium Tee
$17.99

like flowers returning
Premium Tee
$16.99

MTHU Records Class white
Premium Tee
$18.99

MTHU Records 2020 LOGO
Premium Tee
$18.99

MTHU designs on premium t-shirts starting at $16.99 to sport your love for vaporwave and help keep projects like these alive.

"Every time I go out with my Anti Vapor Vaporwave shirt I feel like I'm part of something cooler than I am"

Grab some on Teespring!
https://teespring.com/stores/musics-the-hang-up

*Available in various colors and sizes

Outstanding Design Award

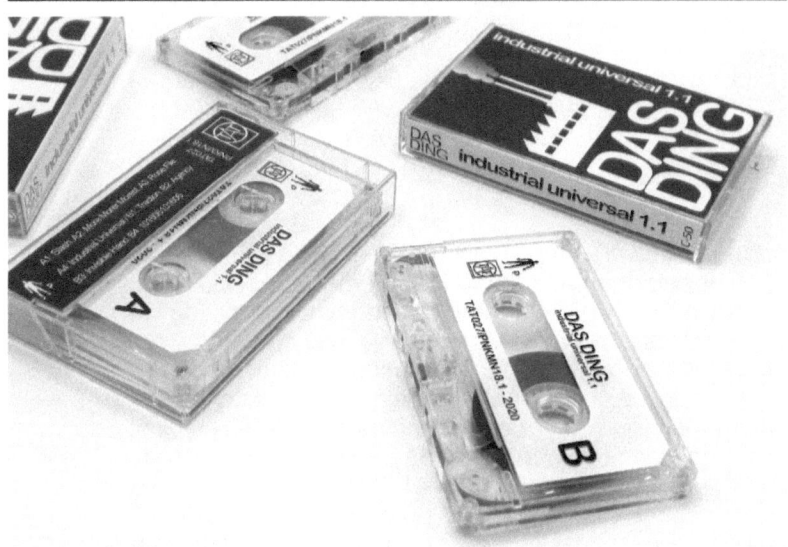

Album: Industrial Universal 1.1 by Das Ding

Lately, I've been getting into the minimal side of techno and found this incredible Netherlands based label, *Pinkman*, that releases some of the most underground sounds. Back in July, they released this cassette pack with social industrial EBM that I knew I had to grab a copy.

The label describes the album as, "Industrial Universal 1.1 adds an extra turmoil and energy into the already time tested cocktail, delivered in Das Dings style." And some how the design of this cassette captures the imagination with minimalistic blue and silver design. A smoke stack factory taking up more than half the cover and a rounded ends of DAS DING to almost say, don't worry, the corporate world will take care of you while the smoke clouds your lungs. Then to throw it all together, the tape liner is blood red in a clear cassette shell hidden by the j-card, making this my favorite design of the month and awarding it the *2nd Visual Signals Outstanding Design Award*.

I used an app & now my 🩶 hurts

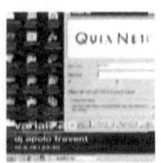

TAKE A GOOD LOOK AT THE DARK AND HOLLOW SHELL MY SOUL USED TO BE IN (VARIAL720 DJ MIX) BY DJ APOLO TREVENT

Although this album is a mix for Varial720's radio show back in 2018, it couldn't have found it at a better time. DJ Apolo Trevent is known for his atmospheric ambience while mixing with the purest of vaporwave and this DJ mix has it all. But what hit me here was just putting on this 30 minute experience and closing my eyes as I work through the pain of a stupid dating app. The title of the album grabbed me the most as it felt like just yesterday I was painting dreams of a possible future with someone and now today am not fit for it.

I am a believer that if I work on being the person I know I want and should be, I will attract someone who is looking to have me in their life. There is someone out there actively looking for me. And some how this was her for 2 weeks. Everything I did while doing my 1 year stint were exact traits she was looking for in a relationship. All the self growth I went through, all the projects I developed, all the art I created, all of me. She liked me for me…

She had some moral(?) differences that I couldn't budge on and in the end left me thinking about my responses to her topics for a week straight. I'm over it now but that was the first time attempting to date in over 6 months. I'm not good at the heartbreak side of these things.

Corona App dating sucks lol, *"all I do is miss you cry myself to sleep…"*

Listen: https://sephorabrainvibes.bandcamp.com/track/take-a-good-look-at-the-dark-and-hollow-shell-my-soul-used-to-be-in-varial720-dj-mix

40

your memory, your soldier

By Yuchi // 清欢

Running along the road last night, she hit upon some strange ideas. They were not exactly ideas, but more like a tumble through memories that had been dissolved and stored in specific smells, lights, and temperatures.

She often encountered this feeling suddenly. Sometimes, when she was half-heartedly wandering off in the direction of the nearest store where any kind of smell would show up without warning, she would feel something like a cramp inside of her chest, perhaps it was her heart, followed by a sense of falling or even a burning feeling in the stomach. That was the moment when it would cross her mind.

It is nothing but a cliché to claim that someone experienced déjà vu. She agreed with that like anybody else who worshiped science. But sometimes, when her feelings got more fleshed out in living color, she had to wonder whether they were just something from her psyche, planted by something she read— or maybe, her dreams.

The more suspicious the explanation, the more it fueled her imagination. The latest one just cropped up on the road she'd ran on numerous times. She believed that the ways of storing memories were various. If memory was a kind of substance like a particle which can be divided into smaller pieces, so that it can't be seen through human eyes but can be concealed in the chinks of the curtains made out of odors, colors, sounds, or even temperatures.

Maybe they were like your special agents or soldiers who were dispersed in countless tiny worlds, chased and slaughtered by ruthless time. Luckily, most of them were cunning enough to escape and hide from the annihilation. They will make their own living and travel incognito until you run across each other again, by which they once again gain the slim chance of hope to light the fuse of memories. Peng! You remembered all of them. That was that moment.

Fidelity of the Reconstructed Beam

By Eric Roy

Labelscar, labelscar, can't make out who you are
—Lord & Taylor, JC Penny, Sakowitz or Sears?
Corndog Craftory still exists! But Orange Julius
turned into a Magic Wok before it disappeared.

Chess King long deposed. Journeys come to its end.
Now that the Gold Mine's gone, can I spend these
arcade tokens at the food court carousel? A man
stands over there, alone—attendant or Musion

Eyeliner? If only Dream Merchant had survived.
We could buy cloves again, the *Necronomicon*,
Malignant Altar shirts for our grateful mothers
to bury in the trash once we move back in.

This is 1986, this is 1994. This is 2666, the Great
American Mall of Life Support, where
clear elevator IVs deliver air-conditioned oxygen
to each phantom wing and liminal leg of every floor.

Where the X now means: nobody's here.
Where the line between metal steps still
grows alien bright right at the end, escalates
into an afterlife only the janitor has ever seen.

Modern Gran Turismo Feels

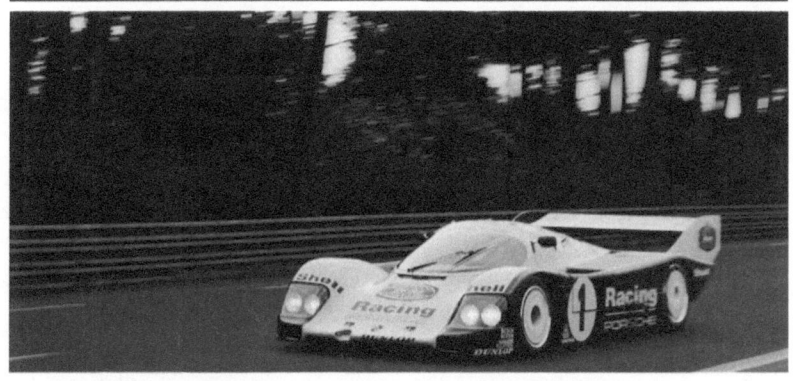

(Above) part of the 1985 by urbanite with a cat album

I recently had a chat with *urbanite with a cat* AKA *Saury*, to find out more about their new GT influenced side project.

1. What inspired you to start the urbanite with a cat project? what are the influences?
"Because I met 3R2 who is a professional musician in Taiwan. That makes me think I should try to make some original stuff. I want to make tracks sounds like GT OST, so 3R2 recommend me a retro VST M1."

2. What's your favorite Gran Turismo game?
"GT Sport (after 7 release, it may be my new favorite)
    *GT4 is my first GT series game, and yellow EVO V is my first dream car"

3. What DAW do you use to make music?
"FL Studio. most of tracks are made with Korg M1 VST"

4. Are you an initial D fan and if so, what's your favorite stage and what character do you relate to.
"yes, Third Stage. i like Ryosuke Takahashi"

5. If you could have a dream car from the 80s or 90s what would it be?
"Honda NSX (first generation)"

Aug - Sept Weather Reports

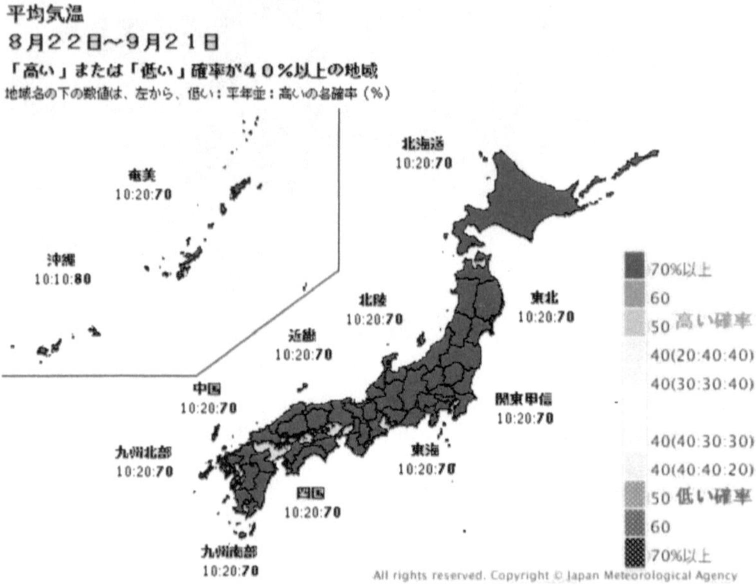

北海道
10:20:70

奄美
10:20:70

沖縄
10:10:80

北陸
10:20:70

東北
10:20:70

近畿
10:20:70

中国
10:20:70

関東甲信
10:20:70

九州北部
10:20:70

東海
10:20:70

四国
10:20:70

九州南部
10:20:70

70%以上
60
50 高い確率
40(20:40:40)
40(30:30:40)
40(40:30:30)
40(40:40:20)
50 低い確率
60
70%以上

地図上をクリックすると各地方の詳しい予報がご覧いただけます。　1か月予報は毎週木曜日14時30分、3か月予報は毎月25日頃14時、暖候期予報は2月、寒候期予報は9月の3か月予報と同時に発表します。　このページの予報は、発表時刻から地方毎に順次更新されます。季節予報が発表された地方でも更新されるまでは前回発表の内容が表示されますので、季節予報の内容の確認は、1か月予報は14時40分以降、3か月予報・暖候期予報・寒候期予報は14時10分以降に全国の予報が完全に更新されてからお願いいたします。

One-month and three-month forecasts are issued at 14:30 JST every Thursday and at 14:00 JST around the 25th of each month respectively. Warm- and cold-season outlooks are issued in February and September respectively in concurrence with three-month forecasts. This months predictions are in the 70%

The Rise, Revival and The New Era of Dreampunk

By Z.E.R.O // @iamZEROmusic

Recently, we're currently experiencing a fantastic moment in the vaporwave (and derivatives) history. The revival and new era of Dreampunk.

The term "Dreampunk" was first presented for us with the rise of the classic Dream Catalogue, owned by HKE (F.K.A. Hong Kong Express), at the time using the term as a Bandcamp Album Tag since their first release. But then, how did this little tag start to create its own identity?

Dreampunk created its own identity when two masterminds in 2014 decided to combine their forces. We're talking about the legendary collaboration between Hong Kong Express and t e l e p a t h テレパシー能力者, 2814.

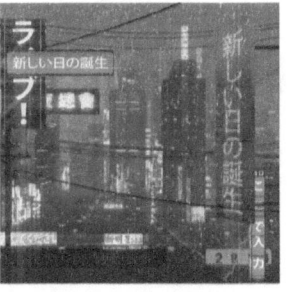

Debuting on October 25th of 2014, a self titled album was released through Ailanthus Recordings and it was an impact that no one was expecting, mainly because the project "broke the rules" being a completely original and kinda futuristic album. Even that the self titled album was a huge impact, no one was ready for what would be released on January 21st of 2015. The absolute classic and historical album titled '新しい日の誕生 (Birth of A New Day).

For many, Birth of A New Day is the essential of Dreampunk. Striking pads and melodies, pianos with long reverbs and unforgettable synths. That's where Dreampunk created the own identity. From there, Dream Catalogue would take a direction that would follow this same pattern until the rise of the 'Flap' genre on the label.

Meanwhile, it created an incredible and really devoted community, and right when we thought that the genre would be forgotten, two mysterious labels were reviving it on the underground way.

One of these names that come into mind when thinking about the revival of this mysterious genre is the game-changing, VILL4IN. VILL4IN is a mysterious record label that according to their Bandcamp description is residing in somewhere at Shenzhen, China, starting officially with a really interesting concept of releases and different catalog series: VOID, MANA, CNCT, DUSK, CCCP and NOIR Series, each one with its own style and identity.

When asked about people calling out Dreampunk as a Vaporwave sub-genre, they said that "Vaporwave is a good blanket term for new-age experimental music (including dreampunk, slushwave, and many others) because everyone has their own definition of what 'vaporwave' is supposed to be. [...] BTW I could easily call dreampunk a sub-genre of IDM and there will be people who believe it. In any case, Dreampunk is so married with the vaporwave crowd that at this point the discussion will never end."

On the other hand, another label that also was still releasing dreampunk
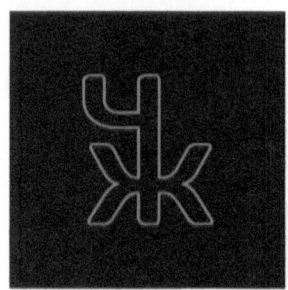 in the undergrounds, we have the incredible project by CMD094 and Panta Rhei, Pure Life Tapes. Pure Life Tapes is a label that releases incredible dreamy and "pure" music on Bandcamp and SoundCloud.

In an interview for the Dreampunk Record Club, Panta Rhei said that "Dreampunk as a movement has gone through a much-needed period of self-reflection and separation from vaporwave. Seb's video on Dreampunk and LIVEWIRE were definitely big factors in that. I think it's been long overdue and it's helped several artists find their community and labels find their identity".

In a Twitter conversation with the founder of the Dreampunk Record Club group, Blissm0nkey, one of the biggest Dreampunk enthusiasts on the internet, said that Dreampunk "Has been described as an evolution of the film soundtrack with an emphasis on creating atmospheres that illuminate imagination, release emotions, and create a space to escape from all the familiar ways we experience ourselves". Also, when asked about how it feels to listen to Dreampunk, Blissm0nkey said that "The genre evokes references to really powerful stuff like feelings of release from intense emotions or escape from the human condition. Others refer to engaging in private reveries, internal narratives, or dreamlike atmospheres, all based [in the] the artist's cues and techniques."

Dreampunk was and still is a really promising future for the ambient, dreamy and cyberpunk musicians out there and just like Future Funk and other genres, Dreampunk has been following its own path holding hands together with Vaporwave, but already with its own identity, essence and history. The Dreampunk movement will possibly never die and since this recent revival, I won't expect it ending soon.

围棋 (go) Full Game Kifu

Date : 2018-10-06
WhitePlayer : 围棋窗
WhiteRank : 18k
Komi : 6.5

BlackPlayer : JacquesBtmn13
BlackRank : 17k
Result : W+1.5

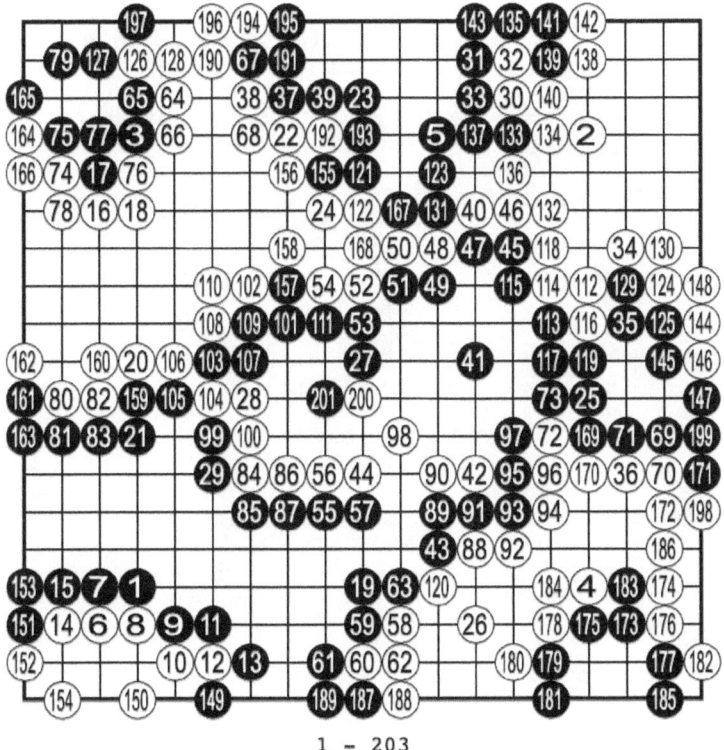

1 - 203

MACINTOSH PLUS 420 MEMES

I admit it, every once in a while I gotta listen to the classic and I love looking at the comments for the memes. Below are some that made me laugh:

We spend our whole life gathering guests for our funeral
/music plays

How does the the human brain ignore the second "the"
/music plays

If your son becomes a priest, do you call him father?
/music plays

Your future self is watching you through your memories
/music plays

When you get a bigger bed, you have more bed room but less bedroom
/music plays

If you wear a sock Inside-out, the whole universe wears it except you
/music plays

In order to not suck, a vacuum has to suck
/music plays

When we wash our hands, we are just watching them wash themselves
/music plays

Do you ever stop and think about how the brain named itself?
/music plays

If you clean your vacuum cleaner, then you're the vacuum cleaner
/music plays

A fish in sea is better than on land because of efficiency
/music plays

Clapping is hitting yourself because you like something
/music plays

When you realize 1980 is closer to World War II than 80s is to today.
/music plays

SOGO // そうご電器 CM1999年

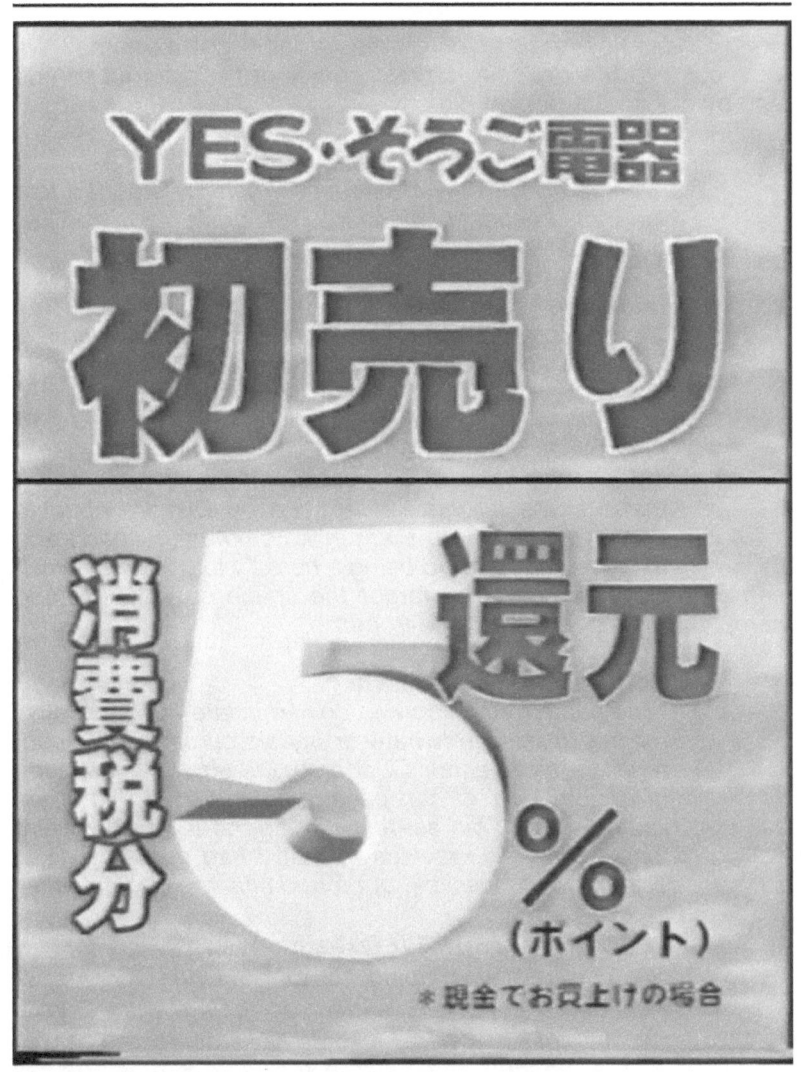

そごう電器全品5%OFF! 炊飯器 (rice cooker)、天ぷら鍋 (deep fryer)、ステンレス製の電気ティーポットなどでナンバーワン!

Behind the Name

Ever wonder how your favorite artist or label got its name? We went out into the deepest darkest corner of the internet to find out.. by asking the person directly~

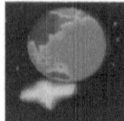

dynamic frequency // @DfDynamic
"i came up with my artist name when my stepdad told me that "frecuencia dinámica" is a great name so i just put it in English and that's the origin of my name."

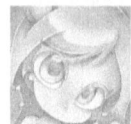

takuchi // @takuchi69
"My nickname when I was a student. The real name is the base. And "takuchi" is all lowercase."

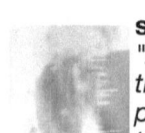

sam bik // @aherointl
"Ahero was kind of a "mistake" if you wanna call it that... I was talking with Hatena on Discord about a person arguing with them in a comments section and they Hatena to "stop being a hero." I told Hatena "yeah man stop being a hero" but forgot the space between 'a' and 'hero,' and that's where it came from!"

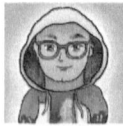

Petridisch // @petridisch
"The name Petridisch was coined in late 2015 as a way for me to release 'whatever' music came to my head, regardless of genre. Of course, there's the implication of a 'petri dish' of musical attempts, also at that time I was also reading a lot of old sci-fi, including the incredibly weird work of Thomas Disch. Previous to that, I had used my given name for projects which was 'ok' but found ultimately a limiter."

クリスタルKITSUNE // @kitsunedesu
"Originally it was going to to be Chris Kitsune or Kurisune(クリスネ). I ended up going with Crystal because of a mix of my favorite Pokémon game as well as the reoccurring crystal in the Final Fantasy games (hence the Final Fantasy esque logo). Kitsune has always been my online alias for everything since fox is my favorite animal!"

NU APOLLO // @nu_apollo

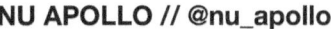

"To be honest I just randomly came up "Nu Apollo" one day while trying to think of some song names. I thought "Nu" sounded pretty cool and vaporwave-esque, and then I thought "Apollo" just fit perfectly. I tried going for a modern/futuristic theme for that name. And then "W.R.I." (World Radio International) came to mind while making my first signalwave album ("分離"). I thought that album sounded like something that would come out of some old abandoned radio station, and so that name came to mind and has stuck with me ever since."

TUPPERWAVE // @TUPPERWAVEMUSIC

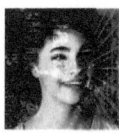

"I needed to change my artist name and I was thinking of a household name. So, I took a look in the cupboard and saw a Tupperware rice maker.
I just mashed Vaporwave and Tupperware together!"

Strawberry Station // @StrawberryStat1

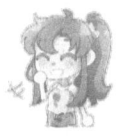

"My stage name was a case of dipping into my interests and favourite things that aren't necessarily music related. Strawberries are my favourite fruit. As for station, my guilty "Otaku" passion is trains, so you'll often find me at one either catching one or just watching them go by! The fact that it sounds cool translated into other languages - イチゴ駅、Gare Fraise, Erdbeere Bahnhof... well that's just a bonus, eh?"

pory // @sk8reel

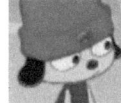

"HATENA came from my love and memories of the old Nintendo DSi and stuff around it. there was this free drawing animation app called Flipnote Studio and it had this online service in connection to a japanese (carrier??) online service called Flipnote Hatena, it comes from that. it shut down i think around 2013 around the same time Nintendo WFC for DS and Wii also shut down, maybe before that. just some cool lil trivia Smiling face with smiling eyes"

Want to know the story behind your favorite artists name? Dm me on twitter @signalsVisual and we'll find out in the next issue!

🌴 1am バイブBlunts

By Jay Wallace // @jaywallace1

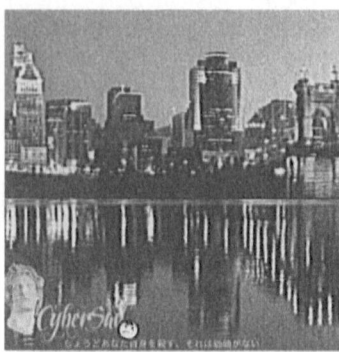

JW: What lead to you making dark ambient/ambient/Vaporwave?

1amblunts: Creating, expressing, feeling, the culmination of ourselves is part of the experience. Often attracting spirits as ourselves. Was it meant to be?

JW: What do you consider yourself, an ambient artist, an experimental artist, a Vaporwave artist?

1amblunts: I guess if I had to label myself something it would just be experimental. I wouldn't consider myself an artist, or really anybody. I'm just here.

JW: Is 1amblunts your only alias?

1amblunts: 1am is not my only alias. The rest are best kept secret.

JW: Out of your work, what is your favorite album?

1amblunts: I like Eternal Exodus 2. A blend of sounds to numb to.

JW: Let's talk about Evening Disclosure. (eveningdisclosure.bandcamp.com) What is it? Are you a founder, or are you just a contributing member? What is Evening Disclosure's mission statement, if there is one?

1amblunts: An empty stage for all and any performers. Founded under a group, I am the primary operator. E.D. is a place of expression, a doorway to different dimensions. Places from afar, and within. Evening Disclosure, the darkest hub world.

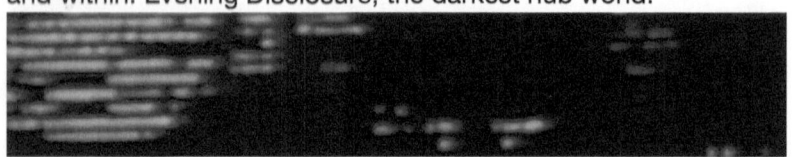

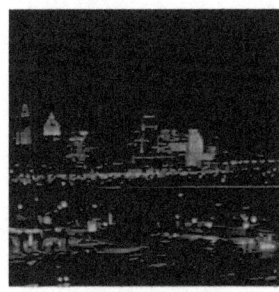

JW: Favorite Evening Disclosure release and why?

1amblunts: The All Alone series. Spectrum of lonely perception. (left)

JW: You've contributed songs to compilations around Bandcamp, such as 3 A.M. for Dark Web Recordings. What has been your favorite comp. album you contributed to?

1amblunts: I don't really have a favorite. It's always interesting to see who else appears on them all. Fidelity Zero has a lot of different people for example.

JW: Have you ever released any of your stuff on cassette?

1amblunts: I've been featured on cassette, but currently have none of my own.

JW: Do you plan to do physical releases in the future, for either 1amblunts or Evening Disclosure?

1amblunts: E.D. has no plans for such right now. 1am will in the future.

JW: Why do you like Vaporwave, Dark Ambient, Plunderphonics and other genres you dabble in?

1amblunts: Like before, it's all an expression. Sometimes I feel like I've gotta extract something from within. Then let it go, like a balloon.

JW: Any releases coming up?

1amblunts: There will be some things here and there in the future.

Find 🌴1am バイブBlunts on Bandcamp or Twitter @1amBlunt

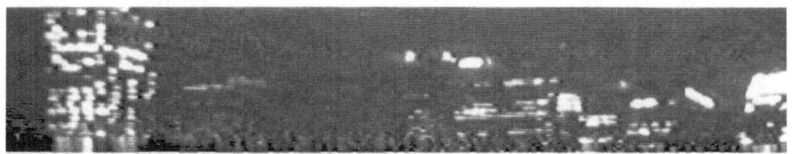

美日都闹疫情「婴儿荒」出生人数将下滑10%

I'm taking Chinese classes online again and in my second class, my teach decided to torment me with translating an entire article into english. All this really taught me was Chinese news outlets put useless sentence into an article to hit SEO marks as much as US bloggers do. Without further ado, I present to you how *Japan, S. Korea and USA won't have enough kids because of Covid.*

美日都闹(nào)疫情(yì qíng)「婴儿荒」出生人数(rén shù)将(jiāng)下滑(xià huá)10%
Epidemics in the U.S. and Japan "A baby shortage" Number born down 10%

日经(rì jīng)新闻报导(bào dǎo)，日本与(yǔ)美国明年的出生人数将下滑10%，因为新冠肺炎(xīn guān fèi yán)疫情(yì qíng)对全球(quán qiú)经济(jīng jì)造成(zào chéng)冲击(chōng jī)，导致(dǎo zhì)年轻人(nián qīng rén)不太敢(gǎn)结婚生子(shēng zǐ)。
A Japanese newspaper reported that Japan's and USA 's births next year will be down 10%. because the coronavirus situation will impact the entire economy, which may lead to young people not wanting to start a family.

第一生命(shēng mìng)经济研究所(yán jiū suǒ)经济学家(jīng jì xué jiā)熊(xióng)野英生预估(yù gū)，明年日本新生儿人数将下滑约10%。去年(qù nián)仅(jǐn)有86万名(wàn míng)新生儿，为追踪(zhuī zōng)这项(xiàng)数据(shù jù)以来(yǐ lái)首次(shǒu cì)低于(dī yú)90万人。
First some research economists predicts, next year Japan's birth rate will be down 10%. Next year will barely have 860k names for children, while last time there were 900k people.

对日本和韩国这两个已面临(miàn lín)严峻(yán jùn)人口(rén kǒu)变化(biàn huà)的亚洲(Yà zhōu)经济体(tǐ)而言(ér yán)，疫情(yì qíng)又对决(duì jué)策(cè)者鼓励(gǔ lì)家庭(jiā tíng)生育(shēng yù)的努力(nǔ lì)，竖起(shù qǐ)新的障碍(zhàng ài)。即便(jí biàn)在疫情(yì qíng)爆发(bào fā)前，亚洲出现最严重(yán zhòng)的老化(lǎo huà)梦魇(mèng yǎn)，就已开始出现。
Japan and South Korean both face grim population change in regards to asia's economy, the epidemic situation plan is to encourage families to give birth, has a lot of new obstacles. Even before the epidemic, asia currently has an old age problem, and was already on the rise.

雄野英生表示，非正式(fēi zhèng shì)员工(yuán gōng)的工作流(gōng zuò liú)失(shī)等(děng)因素(yīn sù)造成(zào chéng)的经济困难(kùn nan)，将(jiāng)使(shǐ)不婚不生(bù hūn bù shēng)的年轻人增加(zēng jiā)一段时间(shí jiān)。
They said, unofficially, employee work life is causing people to not marry or have kids.

厚(hòu)生劳动(láo dòng)省(shěng)统计(tǒng jì)，日本5月结婚对数为32,544对，较去年同期骤降(zhòu jiàng)三分之二，去年这个时间会有许多(xǔ duō)人结婚，是因为日本新天皇(tiān huáng)登基(dēng jī)、并迎接令和时代，但今年5月的数字(shù zì)相比(xiāng bǐ)前年5月也少了30%以上。
Japanese May marriage totals were 32,544, comparing that to last year, it has plummeted almost in half, last year had a lot more marriages, (apparently) this is because they have a new emperor of Japan (?). but May of this year compared to May of last year, is fewer than 30% or more (in regards to marriage).

南韩今年4月的结婚对数(duì shù)较去年同期(tóng qī)减少(jiǎn shǎo)20%。
April of this year in South Korea compared to last year marriage has decreased 20%.

日本去年生育(yù)率(lǜ)降(jiàng)至(zhì)12年低(dī)点的1.36。厚(hòu)劳(láo)省(xǐng)资深(zī shēn)官员警告(jǐng gào)说，今明两年的这个数字(shù zì)，将可能进一步(jìn yī bù)下探。
Last year in Japan, birth rate dropped by 1.36 in 12 months. A senior official from the Ministry of Labour and Welfare warned, the number for this year and the next will be one step lower.

然而(rán ér)，这样(zhè yàng)的衰减(shuāi jiǎn)不局限(bù jú xiàn)于亚洲。华府(Huá fǔ)智库(zhì kù)布鲁金斯研究院(yán jiū yuàn)报告指出，美国明年的出生人数，可能比今年少30万至(zhì)50万人。用美国每年平均(píng jūn)出生370万人来计算(jì suàn)，相当于(xiāng dāng yú)减少(jiǎn shǎo)10%。

However, this isn't just in Asia. Washington, D.C.'s brookings.edu (a research institute) points out, American next year birth rate numbers could be around 300k to 500k fewer people. Using American's yearly average birth rate (3.7 million people in total) compared to this statistic, we will see a 10% decrease.

这份报告(bào gào)指出(zhǐ chū)，「一个持续(chí xù)较深远(shēn yuǎn)的衰退(shuāi tuì)，对有些人而言(ér yán)，意味(yì wèi)较低的终生(zhōng shēng)收入(shōu rù)，不仅(jǐn)让部分(bù fen)女性延后(yán hòu)生育，也让他们决定(jué dìng)少生小孩」。
This report points out because of a recession, some people will have a lower lifetime income, and delaying childbirth allows women to decide to have fewer children.

有史(shǐ)为鉴(jiàn)，经济危机(jīng jì wēi jī)期间(qī jiān)的出生人数会衰减(shuāi jiǎn)。根据(gēn jù)布鲁金斯研究院(yán jiū yuàn)，2008年金融(róng)海啸(hǎi xiào)带来(dài lái)的不景气(bù jǐng qì)，是美国少生约(yāo)40万人的其中(qí zhōng)一个因素(yīn sù)。
History shows during economic crises, birth rates will decline. According to Brookings, the 2008 recession caused 400K fewer births in the USA.

在全球(quán qiú)蔓延(màn yán)对工(duì gōng)作与收入(shōu rù)的担忧(dān yōu)之际(zhī jì)，年轻人已受到(shòu dào)沉重(chén zhòng)的打击。国际(guó jì)劳工(láo gōng)组织(zǔ zhī)线上(xiàn shàng)调查(diào chá)发现(fā xiàn)，在全球18-29岁的年龄(nián líng)层中，有17.1%的人表示自疫情(yì qíng)爆发(fā)以来就未(wèi)工作过，就连(lián)仍(réng)在工作的人，工时也缩减(suō jiǎn)23%，进而(jìn ér)拖累(tuō lěi)收入(shōu rù)。
When one has to worry about work and income, young people across the globe are affected. A ILO survey found 17.1% of 18-29 year olds around the world have not worked since the outbreak and even those who are working are reducing their hours by 23% and are seeing lower income.

This took about 3 hours, so I hope you find some value from it.

Fan Collection

by Mulletovich // @mulletovich

Collecting Vaporwave shirts and merch all started with joining the George Clanton Fan club. Knowing that buying shirts and Merch was direct funding to 100% Electronica made it one of the best things I could do.

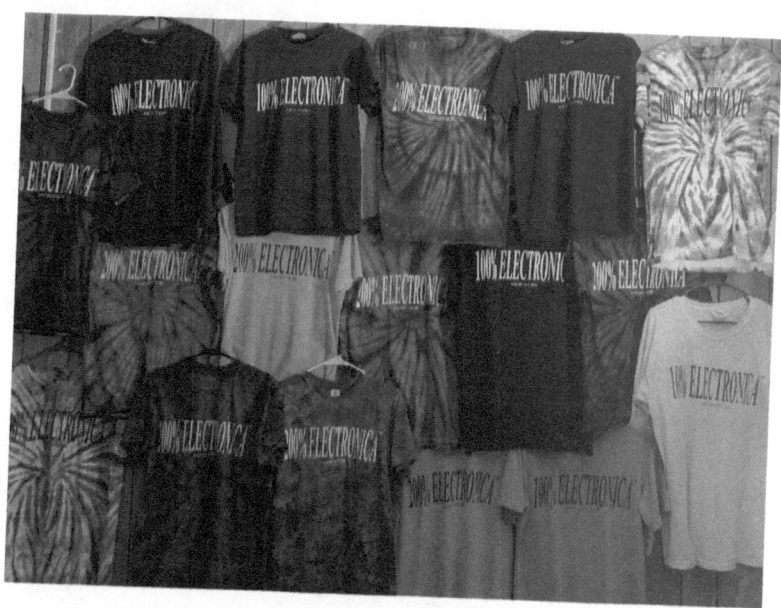

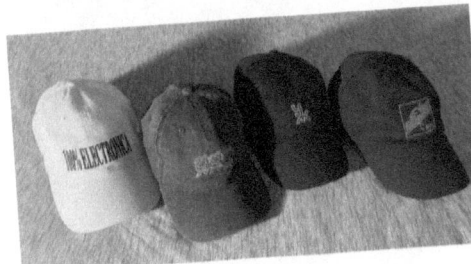

As I learned more about vaporwave and other music labels from within, I started to collect more to help support and give more exposure. Help fuel the underground scene.

Finally Vaporwave artists, many who I call friend. Seeing everyone reach their dreams and continue to be creative made owning shirts and etc that much more meaningful.

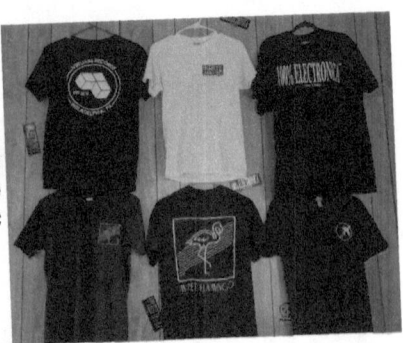

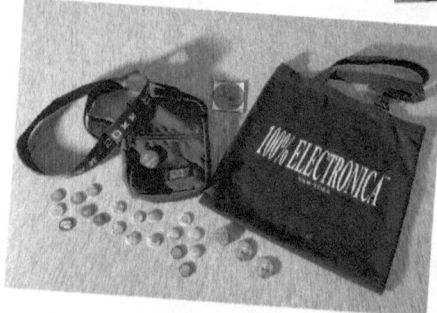

Also rumor has it after acquiring a shirt from EQUIP, R23x, Deaths Dynamic Shroud and Vaperror it will summon the majestic Long sleeve shirt of Neo Gaia Legend Crossed swords (Artists shirts)

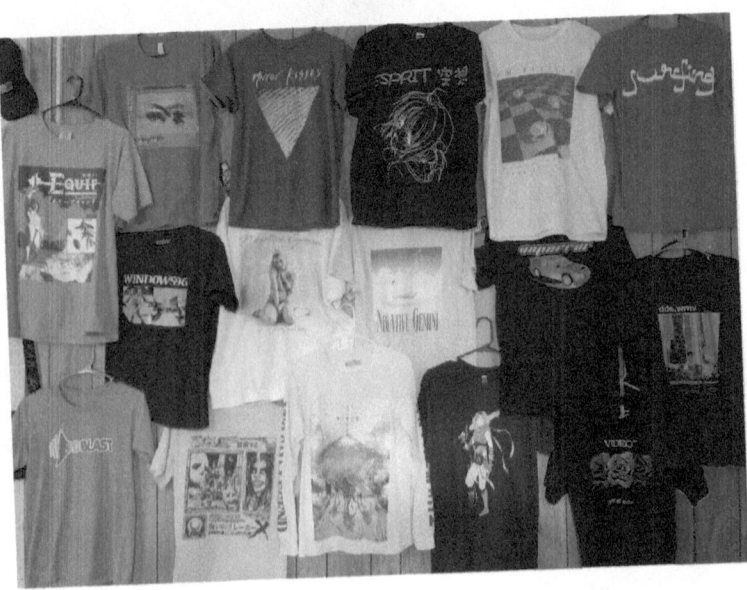

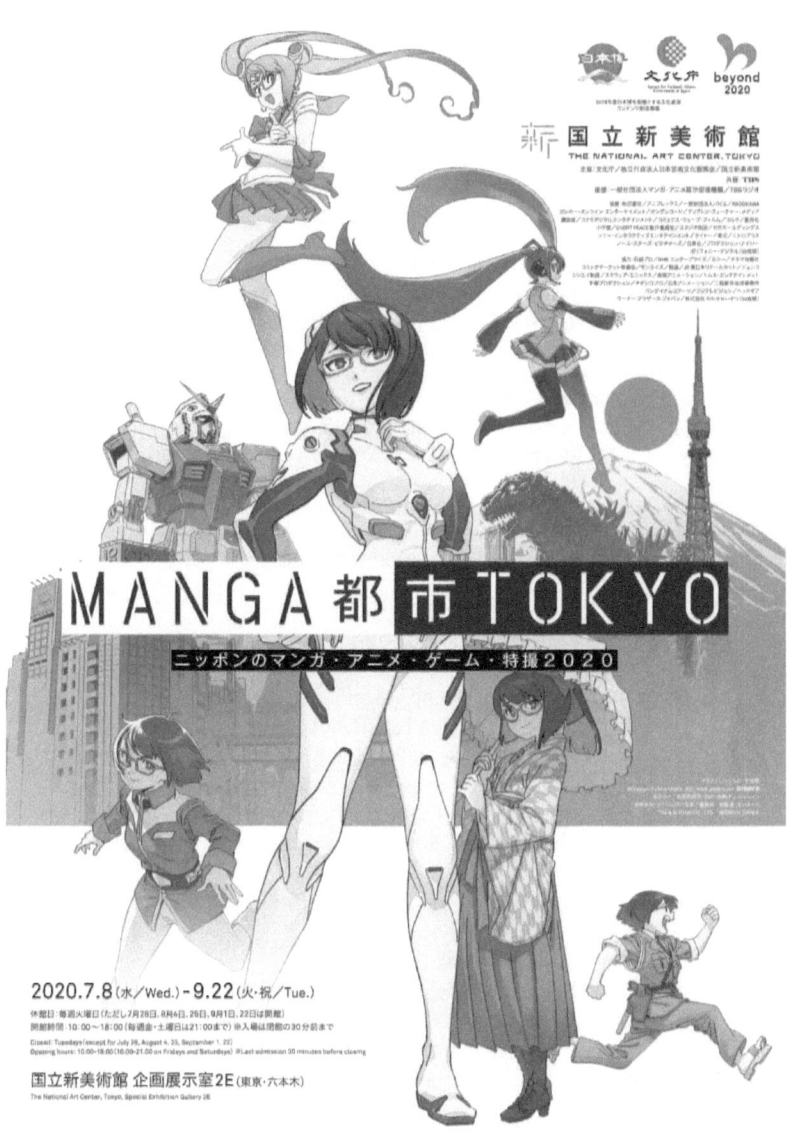

開催期間 2020.8.12（水/Wed）〜11.3（火・祝/Tue）
Buy Tickets: https://manga-toshi-tokyo.jp/ticket/

physical signals

After going through that whole App dating fiasco, it made me realize, I have a lot of emotional trauma I need to work on. Back in Shenzhen, I used to go to a weekly meditation class and ended up becoming friends with the teacher, Varoon. We even ended up going to India together for a couple of weeks.

I reached out to him for some thoughts on what I was going through and he offered for me to start a meditation program. A 41 day program. Because of it, I've totally restructured my life around the exercise mainly because it requires me to wake up at 5am, every morning… including weekends. I'm 3 weeks into it and as of this latest week, I've got a pretty solid schedule I've been following. I don't know how long this will be part of my life, so I just want to document what my days look like.

I live alone, in a brand new city during covid. This might be the only chance I get to be this rigorous on my self-discipline and growth, so I am finding a lot of enjoyment in pushing my mind and body to it's limits.

5:05am: instantly get out of bed

5:06am - 5:35am: morning yoga
- 6 sets of Surya Namaskara (sun salutation) yoga
- Nadi Shodhana Pranayama balancing breathing technique (left nose, right nose alternated breathing)
- Butterfly stretching
- Meditation with awareness between eyebrows

5:25am - 6:00am: shower / brush teeth

*6:00am - 6:50/7:00am:
- If I have morning Chinese classes, I video call for 1 hour with my teacher
- If I do not, I am currently studying the book, "Subtle Wisdom" by Master Sheng-yen

7:00am - 3:00pm: Full-time job
- 11:00am: I'll some times eat lunch for 30 minutes while working

3:00pm - 3:30pm: Relax on the computer or distract myself from work troubles

3:30pm - 4:00pm: MTHU, work on Visual Signals, etc (some form of side project work)

4:00pm - 5:00pm: prepare dinner and eat while watching some Chinese news, TV show or work on Visual Signals.

5:00pm - 6:00pm: Chinese studies

6:00pm - 7:00pm: Take a 45 minute nap then get ready for bed

7:00pm - 9:00pm: Chinese classes with two different teachers

9:00pm - 5:05am: sleep

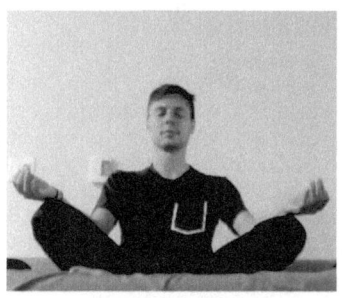

Additionally, there are some extra living habits that are required. First, all meals must be vegetarian. I've been at that game for 7 years, so that was easy. I must practice celibacy for the duration of the program (NO FAP GANG!). I find this rather easy tbh, but it isn't my first time doing this kind of thing.

Additionally, it was recommended to drink a *gulp* of water every hour and take a few breaths to center oneself. So to make this easier, my phone literally has an alarm at every hour of the day. This is how I am able to manage my schedule so cleanly. I've found taking the deep breath and focusing outside of my mind during work has been a tremendous benefit. Plus, I know I'm getting more than enough water intake.

In the end this is what it boils down to. I am stuck in my head. I get very obsessed with doubts and personal fears. It ruins me at times and I'm looking for anything that can help me grow and manage it. I know it's my mind not treating my kindly. I need to help nurture it and this has helped me focus on something else besides myself.

If this is something you're interested, my teacher has started an NGO in India. His company is in the works of building a meditation/yoga retreat center on land he owns. For more information feel free to checkout this website: https://mooladharayoga.org

Mirror of My Mind

By Seabaud // @seabaud

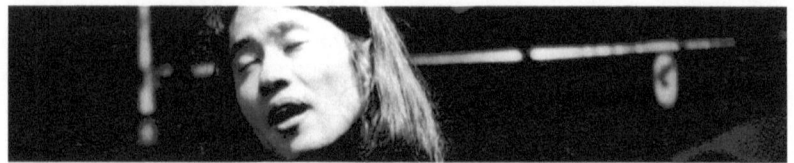

A conversation with Ryo Kawasaki

With its tableau of washed out synths and speed-ramped samples vaporwave captures the spirit of the past with an imagined retrospective. Along the ride as we cast a gaze into the rearview mirror let's consider what the electronic music producer landscape was during the 80s and 90s.Â

Join me in a return to the pre-MIDI era as we chat with Ryo Kawasaki, world renowned jazz fusion guitarist and electronic music pioneer. Ryo was born in 1947 in the Koenji neighborhood of Western Tokyo. His early introduction to music would serve as the inspiration for electronic music exploration leading to building synthesizers and developing music software for the Commodore 64 home computer.

"When I was 5 years or so, my father gave me a toy piano with a songbook as a Christmas present and it was indeed great fun for me to playing on it. So I guess that was the inspiration for me to develop software something like that for children along with my knowledge or analog synthesis. I was also kinda electrics wiz in my childhood so that I could literally build anything"

This experience paved the way for Ryo to expand the possibilities of making analog synthesis to everyone. When Roland introduced their GR-500 guitar synthesizer module in the late 1970s he immediately started to modify both guitar and synth module to create a handbuilt mobile
guitar synthesis system with the assistance or complete schematics for Roland. His early electronic electronic music compositions integrated both his signature synth guitar sound and drum machine programming.

"All these rhythm tracks were programmed by myself on sequencer. During 1981-1983 there was no MIDI sampler, so they were programmed using pulse wave sync among different rhythm machines and orchestrated with my guitar synthesizer sounds"

When home computing hit the scene in the 1980s the unique sounds of the Commodore 64 and itsÂ SID chip (Sound Interface Device) attracted musicians across the world including Ryo, now living in New York City. He took a deep dive into developing his own music production software: Kawasaki Synthesizer (1984) Kawasaki Rhythm Rocker (1984) Kawasaki Magical Musiqcuill (1985) and Kawsaki MIDI workstation (1986)

"One thing I didn't know when I put my hands on the Commodore 64 was programming languages. So I spend a couple of years to develop my machine language skill, because that was the only way I could develop the software that I envisioned. Basically to enable real time playing over computer keyboard to turn computer into musical instrument. I remember is that I was spending an average 16 hours a day just to learn programming and develop software during 1983-1985 or so. And I have a gap without any new album release between 1983-1986 while I was releasing average two new albums every year before and after. So I guess I have isolated myself from musical performances and recording career during that time."

Many of today's electronic music producers can thank Ryo for introducing them to the computer as an instrument and production tool. Ryo's software was designed with an emphasis on simplicity making it easy for beginners to explore synthesis and composition.

"It all comes down to API especially the most important thing is to develop perfect human/user interface. How to input request or order and how to output the answer or result instantaneously without any effort, confusion or delay, especially for musical instrument because people notice any delay longer that 16 milliseconds as audible and physical delay that cannot be tolerated in this type of software and everything must be intuitive without need for reading user's manual to use given software, anyway that's most important point of view as software designer to develop useful tool as simple as how to use umbrella or how to put your shoes on"

His software is remembered for it's dynamic animations that leveraged the Commodore's MOS Technology VIC-II graphics chip.

"As for Rhythm Rocker, it was kind of was kind of fun idea to incorporate computer graphic effect along with music as to be a bit more theatrical and animated effect to be enjoyed, a bit more inclined to gaming software kind of feel"

Ryo returned to music composition in the late 1980s producing house music under his own music label Satellites Records. His own software remained at the heart of his studio as his 12" dance singles became staples of the club scene.

"After 1986 all those tracks were programmed using my own development called Kawasaki MIDI Workstation program and utilizing various sample sounds to make the entire arrangement/ orchestration myself. Basically all of those tracks you hear in my one man band except featured instruments or vocals on top of my programmed rhythm track and arrangements."

Throughout these decades of innovation, Ryo maintained his passion for jazz. As a guitar sideman he performed with the likes of Gil Evans, Elvin Jones and Chico Hamilton. When the time arrived to explore new jazz territory he left New York City and moved to Europe. This marked his departure from electronic music. His most recent ensemble called Level 8 performed this jazz composition "Jazz Ballet: Still Point" with ballet dances from the Estonian National Opera House.

"After 2000 I move from New York City to Tallinn, Estonia. I have completely abandoned and stopped producing music with use of programmed rhythm tracks, sampled sounds or synthesizer. Simply because they sound obsolete and dated to me and returned to perform and record music only using live musicians. I've performed at Cotton Club Japan for 6 concerts during summers with my Estonian Level 8 band but this is my new jazz rock band with live musicians focusing on my compositions and sound. I am more inclined to further develop 60s and 70s music approaches and sound with live band because to me that's my roots as well as to me it was the highest point for creative and/ or improvisational music in history and I'm not so interested in music developed thereafter unity this day at this point of my own development.

Ryo embodied an unpredictable musical journey. His exploration into disparate sonic territory left us questioning where his music would guide us. Let the "obsolete" sounds he created along the way be an inspiration to vaporwave producers and listeners alike. Ryo wanted to inspire a generation of computer music producers. Let's show him what we can do.

ご冥福をお祈りいたします
川崎 燎
Kawasaki Ryo
1947 - 2020

Playing Vaporwave

By Matt Christodoulou // @vibex_

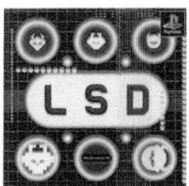 While it predated the birth of vaporwave, *LSD: Dream Emulator* is prime example of the genre. The mixture of repeating patterns, eclectic videography, procedurally-generated soundscapes, and absurdist gameplay trap players in a truly dream-like space. Players are left perpetually uncomfortable but compelled to find a purpose in a purposeless world.

More of a meme than anything else, *Mall Quest* tosses players into the world of Macintosh Plus's Floral Shoppe. While the game itself isn't particularly good, it is a perfect example of how vaporwave can benefit young game designers. Vaporwave's liberal use of asset theft and repurposing empowers designers to create and experiment on a shoestring budget.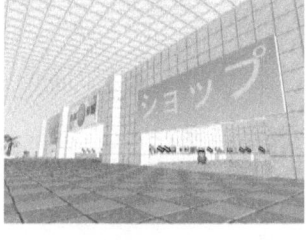

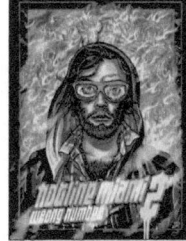 *Hotline Miami* and *Hotline Miami 2: Wrong Number* draw inspiration from the neon lights and disconcerting atmosphere of vaporwave. It marries vaporwave's VHS culture with a brutally violent narrative to create a truly unique experience. Don't expect an easy go of it though —this game is just as cruel to you as it is to its characters.

四色 *(Shishoku)* is my own take on a simple vaporwave game. Accompanied by some of Stevia Sphere's elevator music, players color in various geometric shapes in accordance with the four color 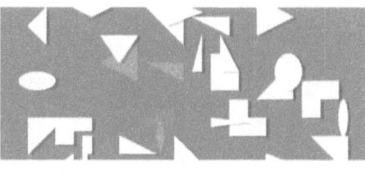 map theorem. As with most of the games here, the goal is simply to enjoy the atmosphere. I hope you enjoy playing it as much as I enjoyed making it.

@musicsthehangup Circles

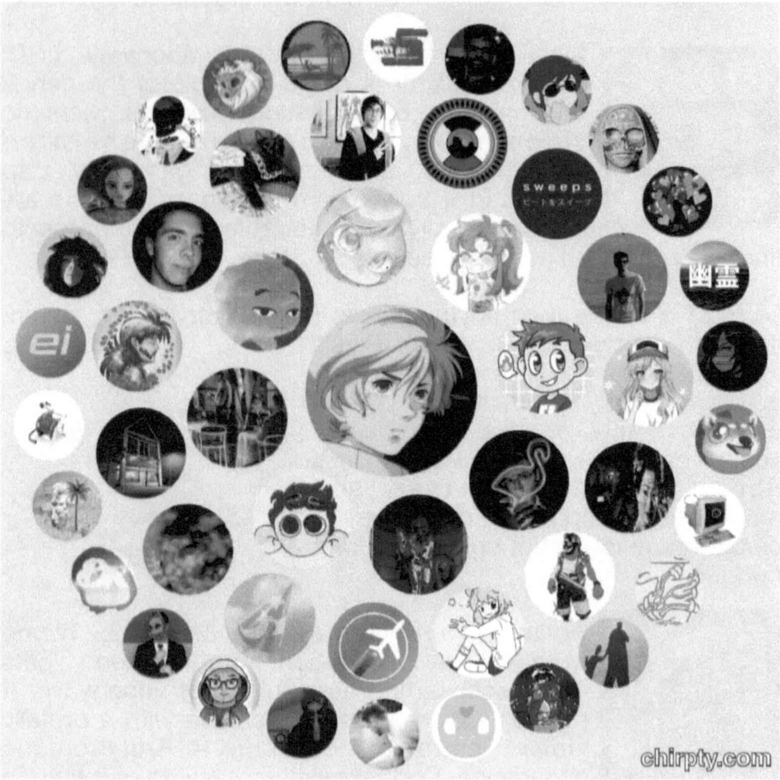

![circles collage]

chirpty.com

Circle 1
@MidClassComfy
@YourUnspeakable
@Pad_Chennington
@n3kkun
@WaveCitizenWave
@takuchi69
@StrawberryStat1
@daydream_deluxe

Circle 2
@kitsunedesu
@firstclasslabel
@badlydrawnhugz
@aherointl
@Donor_Lens
@mulletovich
@jaywallace1
@BooimasterFlex
@fuck_adrianwave
@Chiefahleaf
@sweepsbeats
@virtual_boy_

@snowdreammusic
@maki44875987
@TheCelShade

Circle 3
@yoler0y
@petridisch
@TylerEllis18
@seabaud
@tropicalvirtual
@sute_aca_
@eilogin
@Blissm0nkey
@quintin_q_q
@SleepPattern_AV
@Waterfall2117
@calivibenet
@StachyDj
@vaportorian
@zicoUwU
@Skeletonlipsti1
@Assonance16
@trashgh0st

@mr_oceanmusic
@nicky_mir
@conceptsbot
@ccchristtt
@blashy101
@nighttempo
@aloecityrecords
@Jake_Hanrahan

^ the real 温 crew

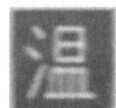

Issue Credits

All article / concepts / diagrams / ads / etc were developed by KITE0080 unless otherwise stated.

Note:
Every artist, label, project, album, opinion, thought, tweet, post, blog, YouTube video, others thoughts or anything in between is not my opinion. Every one of these things belong to the respective artist / label / writer. I don't know what horrific thing someone might say in the future either. Visual Signals, MTHU or KITE0080 are not liable for such future unknown conflicts.

「MANGA都市TOKYO」is not a sponsor, I just wanted to promote it.

Credits:
- All logos / brands / album art belong to their respective owners
- "Hyperconsumersim by Harsh Noise Mall" by Jay Wallace
- "FOMO" by maki
- "Fan Collection" by Mulletovich
- "Mirror of My" Mind By Seabaud
- "Fidelity of the Reconstructed Beam" by Eric Roy // @RobertEricRoy
    - Bio: Eric Roy has poetry forthcoming at Third Coast, Salamander, Bennington Review, Westerly, and Sugar House Review. His poem 'It's Okay To Have Long Hair Long After Middle Age' won the KGB Monday Night Poetry Series annual open reading competition. He lives in Brooklyn, but his home is in Houston, TX.
    - More Poetry: https://nyq.org/poets/poet/ericroy
- "Tape Collection" by Eric Roy
- "Waifu Radio 2 Review" by Nekkun
- "your memory, your soldier" by Yuchi
- "The Rise, Revival and The New Era of Dreampunk" by Z.E.R.O
- "Playing Vaporwave" by Matt Christodoulou
- "Mirror of My Mind" By Seabaud

Official Visual Signals:
- Twitter: @SignalsVisual
- Website: http://visualsignals.xyz

Contact KITE0080 // MTHU
- Twitter: @musicsthehangup // @SignalsVisual
- Instagram: @musicsthehangup
- Website: http://musicsthehangup.com
- Email: contact@musicsthehangup.com

Join the official MTHU Discord:
- http://musicsthehangup.com/discord

Hey again my Future Friends,

I just wanted to add a massive thank you to everyone who contributed to this issue. I can't believe we had over 10 submissions from interviews, to thoughts, from poems to reviews and so much more. Ideally, Visual Signals was always going to have a hard limit of 50 pages but the submissions kept coming in and I had to start taking out my own articles to get everyone in! But that is how it should be, I don't want Visual Signals to just be about me, it's a community effort and I super appreciate every single one of you who wanted to be apart of it. It means the world to me that we have that platform together.

If someone who wrote something that inspired you, go follow them on twitter, let them know, because their efforts are worth the praise. As alway, thanks everyone who was part of this, including you, the reader!

Cheers,
KITE0080 of MTHU

Cover Art Photography by KITE0080 // John Riselvato of the left side of the massive Shenzhen 深圳市民中心 building

* This issue has updated Sept 20th, 2020 to fix article errors

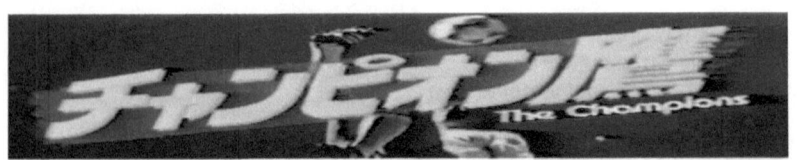

Write for the next issue!

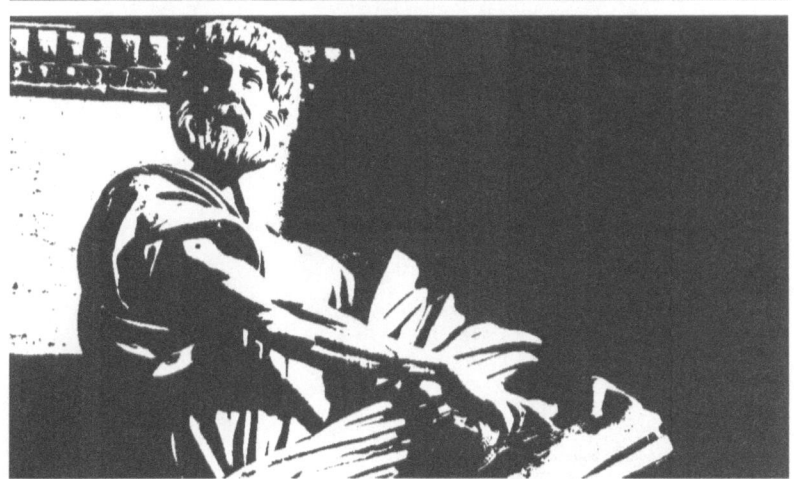

Want to write an article for the next issue? Love vaporwave or internet culture? Got something interesting you want to share? We would love to have you part of the project!

Writing Guidelines:
- Related to the vapor scene, Internet culture or vintage pop culture.

Page Requirements:
- A one-page article without an image must contain a 350 maximum word count
- A one-page article with an image must contain a 275 maximum word count
- A two-page article with two images must contain a less than 600 words
- Images must fall under creative use or belong to you. If art does not fall under creative use, digital editing may be applied or sourcing may be required.

Payment:
If we approve your article, you will receive a free copy of the next Visual Signals issue with your article in it! Monetary payouts are currently unavailable but something I'm working towards.

Contact at:
@signalsVisual on twitter or by email at contact@musicsthehangup.com

Special Shoutout to everyone who reviewed Visual Signals: (ISSUE ZERO) on Amazon. As I promised, here's the reviews you gave and I am super appreciative of it. Want your review in the next issue? Leave a review on Amazon and you too can be featured! (These are always going to be in B&W, sorry to disappoint but I can't sell them at 7.99 USD with color.)

 C. DeBenedetto

⭐⭐⭐⭐⭐ **Love it**

Reviewed in the United States on August 17, 2020

Verified Purchase

I thoroughly enjoyed this. So much more in depth than I expected. Wonderful.

 Alex D

⭐⭐⭐⭐⭐ **Really neat zine**

Reviewed in the United States on August 7, 2020

Verified Purchase

Love this idea. Can't wait for the next issue!

 nathan

⭐⭐⭐⭐⭐ **Wonderful publication**

Reviewed in the United States on August 12, 2020

Verified Purchase

Absolutely wonderfully done magazine found some great artist through the publication, I rlly hope he does a full color one soon

 Pete Z.

⭐⭐⭐⭐⭐ **Amazing book, and a must have companion!**

Reviewed in the United States on August 4, 2020

Having gotten Issue Zero recently. Absolutely stunning books from Music The Hang Ups Kite0080. If you're into vaporwave at all these are must have companions to your vapor experiences. Thank you for all you do mate! Keep being yourself 🍜🍜

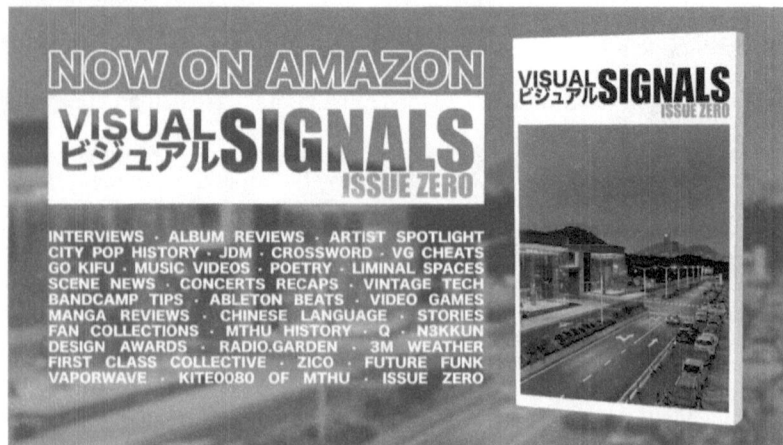

NOW ON AMAZON

VISUAL ビジュアル **SIGNALS** ISSUE ZERO

VISUAL ビジュアル **SIGNALS** ISSUE ZERO

INTERVIEWS · ALBUM REVIEWS · ARTIST SPOTLIGHT
CITY POP HISTORY · JDM · CROSSWORD · VG CHEATS
GO KIFU · MUSIC VIDEOS · POETRY · LIMINAL SPACES
SCENE NEWS · CONCERTS RECAPS · VINTAGE TECH
BANDCAMP TIPS · ABLETON BEATS · VIDEO GAMES
MANGA REVIEWS · CHINESE LANGUAGE · STORIES
FAN COLLECTIONS · MTHU HISTORY · Q · N3KKUN
DESIGN AWARDS · RADIO.GARDEN · 3M WEATHER
FIRST CLASS COLLECTIVE · ZICO · FUTURE FUNK
VAPORWAVE · KITE0080 OF MTHU · ISSUE ZERO